CENTRE FOR EDUCATIONAL RESEARCH

Schooling for Tomorrow

Personalising Education

OECD

ORGANISATION FOR ECONOMIC CO-OPERATION AND DEVELOPMENT

ORGANISATION FOR ECONOMIC CO-OPERATION AND DEVELOPMENT

The OECD is a unique forum where the governments of 30 democracies work together to address the economic, social and environmental challenges of globalisation. The OECD is also at the forefront of efforts to understand and to help governments respond to new developments and concerns, such as corporate governance, the information economy and the challenges of an ageing population. The Organisation provides a setting where governments can compare policy experiences, seek answers to common problems, identify good practice and work to co-ordinate domestic and international policies.

The OECD member countries are: Australia, Austria, Belgium, Canada, the Czech Republic, Denmark, Finland, France, Germany, Greece, Hungary, Iceland, Ireland, Italy, Japan, Korea, Luxembourg, Mexico, the Netherlands, New Zealand, Norway, Poland, Portugal, the Slovak Republic, Spain, Sweden, Switzerland, Turkey, the United Kingdom and the United States. The Commission of the European Communities takes part in the work of the OECD.

OECD Publishing disseminates widely the results of the Organisation's statistics gathering and research on economic, social and environmental issues, as well as the conventions, guidelines and standards agreed by its members.

> *This work is published on the responsibility of the Secretary-General of the OECD. The opinions expressed and arguments employed herein do not necessarily reflect the official views of the Organisation or of the governments of its member countries.*

Publié en français sous le titre :
Personnaliser l'enseignement

Foreword

The aim of "personalising learning" is of growing prominence in thinking and policy discussions on education's future and so is a natural component of CERI's "Schooling for Tomorrow" programme. It springs from the awareness that "one-size-fits-all" approaches to school knowledge and organisation are ill-adapted both to individuals' needs and to the knowledge society at large. The issues go well beyond the directions for school reform itself, as the personalisation agenda is also about promoting lifelong learning and of reforming public services more broadly. The reference to "learning" is important because the agendas reach out well beyond the institutional confines of the places called "schools".

But "personalisation" can mean many things and raises profound questions about the purposes and possibilities for education. For some, it is a natural way forward; for others, it conjures up spectres of learning in isolation or of retreat from schooling as a universal service that fosters social cohesion. The authors in this report have their own interpretations as well as prerequisites of successful implementation.

The importance of airing these issues led to an international seminar – "Personalised Learning: the Future of Public Service Reform" – held in London in May 2004. This relied on the creative partnership of the UK Department for Education and Skills (DfES), and its Innovation Unit in particular, the think-tank Demos, and OECD/CERI. The contributions addressed *inter alia* such questions as the different approaches to personalisation and the policy challenges they raise. What do the learning sciences, including burgeoning research into brain functioning, have to contribute in pointing the way ahead? What role can technology play? What are the constraints imposed by key stakeholders in education systems – including teachers, parents and employers – and how should these be met? The immediate audience was British but the contributors were international and the issues of universal appeal.

The key conference contributions have been elaborated into the chapters that make up this report. It will be complemented by a parallel analysis of educational demand – looking at attitudes, participation and choice in education – to be published in the "Schooling for Tomorrow" series shortly after this one.

Within the OECD, Riel Miller, formerly of the CERI Secretariat, took the main responsibility for launching the work on personalisation, organising the London conference, and working with the experts involved. Detailed editorial contributions in preparing the volume for publication came from consultant Edna Ruth Yahill and from Jennifer Cannon, Delphine Grandrieux, and David Istance. The report is published under the responsibility of the Secretary-General of the OECD.

Anne-Barbara Ischinger
Director for Education

ACKNOWLEDGEMENTS

We here acknowledge the UK Department for Education and Skills (DfES) for its lead in the work on personalisation, including the leadership provided at the time of the London conference by David Miliband and David Hopkins, then Secretary of State for School Standards and Director of the Standards and Effectiveness Unit, respectively. Key intellectual and logistical roles were played by the Innovation Unit at DfES, and especially Directors Mike Gibbons, Valerie Hannon and their team, and by the think-tank Demos and its Director, Tom Bentley. Special thanks go also to international consultant Tony Mackay who chaired the conference on which this volume is based.

We would also like to acknowledge the contribution made by the individual chapter authors, some of whom are mentioned above or in the preface in other capacities: Tom Bentley, William J. Hartley, Yvonne Hébert, David Hopkins, Sanna Järvelä, Charles Leadbeater, David Miliband, Riel Miller, Johan Peter Paludan, Jean-Claude Ruano-Borbalan, and Manfred Spitzer.

Table of Contents

Executive summary

The aim of "personalising learning" is of growing prominence in thinking and policy discussions on education's future and so is a natural component of CERI's "Schooling for Tomorrow" programme. It springs from the awareness that "one-size-fits-all" approaches to school knowledge and organisation are ill-adapted both to individuals' needs and to the knowledge society at large. But "personalisation" can mean many things and raises profound questions about the purposes and possibilities for education. The importance of airing these issues led to an international seminar – "Personalised Learning: the Future of Public Service Reform" – held in London in May 2004 bringing together the UK Department for Education and Skills (DfES), the think-tank *Demos*, and OECD/CERI. The key conference contributions have been elaborated into the chapters that make up this report.

The importance of the personalisation agenda

David Hopkins, who was a Chief Advisor to UK Ministers of Education at the time of the London conference, contributes the report's Introduction. He identifies the foundations of personalisation to be partly historical and social – they importantly reflect people's aspirations and their growing appetite for learning. But he particularly stresses as well the *moral purpose* that drives personalisation. This is seen vividly in conscientious teachers matching teaching to the individual learner, but also in the holistic nature of teachers as a profession working together to equip learners with the proficiency and confidence to pursue understanding for themselves.

Hopkins identifies in the current drive to personalisation the promise of addressing the longstanding constraints on reform and innovation: the limitations imposed by socio-economic variables; those of physical space, and the fact that teachers tend to be responsible for whole groups at any one time; the unsophisticated use of technology and the uniform pace of learning that has traditionally been demanded; the resiliently conservative nature of school organisation, and the step-by-step progression that virtually all children undertake; and the fact that teaching is still not an evidence-based profession.

*Policy strategies to enhance the
personalised learning agenda*

David Miliband, UK Schools Standards Minister at the time of the London conference, presents his vision and policy agenda for personalisation of learning. He places personalisation in the context of "three great challenges". These are: first, that of pursing excellence and equality simultaneously and aggressively; second, how to combine flexibility in delivery with accountability for results; and third, meeting the demand that universal services should have a personal focus. In meeting these challenges, new synergies are needed that depend neither exclusively on market solutions nor on the planned approach.

He outlines five components of personalised learning to guide policy development. i) It needs to be based on detailed knowledge of the strengths and weaknesses of individual students. Hence it must build on assessment for learning and the use of data and dialogue to diagnose every student's learning needs. ii) It calls for the development of the competence and confidence of each learner and so needs teaching and learning strategies that promote this. These include strategies which actively engage all students and which accommodate different speeds and styles of learning. iii) Personalisation means curriculum choice and respect for students, allowing for breadth of study and personal relevance, and clear pathways through the system. iv) Personalisation demands a radical approach to school and class organisation based around student progress. Workforce reform is a key factor, and the professionalism of teachers is best developed when they have a range of adults working with them to meet diverse student needs. v) Personalised learning means the community, local institutions and social services supporting schools to drive forward progress in the classroom. Miliband develops these elements with reference to concrete UK examples.

*Building on research findings on
learning*

Sanna Järvelä, from Finland, reviews research evidence and clarifies key questions relating to personalisation. She distinguishes personalisation from individualisation, on the one hand, and from social learning, on the other, and instead sees it as an approach in educational policy and practice whereby every student matters, and is a route to equalising opportunities through fostering learning skills and motivation.

She examines seven critical dimensions:

- The *development of key skills* which are often domain-specific. Knowledge construction and knowledge sharing form the core processes of learning; and these are connected to the development of higher-order knowledge and skills which are the key organisers for the construction and sharing processes.

- Levelling the educational playing field through the direct improvement of *students' learning skills*. This means teaching students how to analyse, critique, judge, compare and evaluate, and it may be extended to help students think wisely as well as to think well.

- Encouragement of learning through building *motivation*. Motivationally effective teachers make school meaningful cognitively, by enabling students to learn and understand, and motivationally by helping students appreciate its value, especially in potential applications for the knowledge outside school.

- *Collaborative knowledge-building* – new learning environments in education and the workplace are often based on shared expertise. Pedagogical models, tools and practices are being developed to support collaborative learning and reciprocal understanding. She reviews three elements: progressive enquiry, problem-based learning, and project-based learning.

- *New models of assessment* on which personalised learning is seen to depend, such as authentic assessment, direct assessment of performance and digital portfolios.

- Use of *technology* as a personal cognitive and social tool. For the personalisation agenda to succeed, she says, models are needed for the effective use of technology to support individual and social learning. It will call for multi-disciplinary collaboration between educational designers and technology developers and the full exploitation of mobile devices and wireless networks.

- *Teachers* are key: new learning environments require complex instructional designs and teachers will need to be strong in communication and collaboration. It is through them that the above areas will be mediated and promoted, including those of learning skills and new forms of assessment.

Brain research and learning over the life-cycle

Manfred Spitzer (Ulm, Germany) argues that brain research not only shows that we are born for learning and do it for our entire life, but also shows the conditions for successful learning and differences in each stage of life. The time has come, he says, to use this understanding for shaping the learning environments and programmes; we can no longer afford to treat the most important resource that we have, our brain, as if we knew nothing about how it works. Thus, it is important to create the conditions for transferring insights from basic studies of learning in brain research to the practice of teaching.

His discussion is organised around a number of key themes where the burgeoning knowledge base about how the brain functions can inform education and the personalisation agenda. One regards the way young children are able to generate *rules from examples* and how this relates to neurological processes; for instance, when we learn single items (people, places, words, events) the hippocampus is the part of the brain most involved, in contrast with the cortex which is engaged in extracting rules. *Phases, stages and windows* discusses the maturation process and the ways in which the brain is able to come to complexity via the learning of more basic patterns and connections which are not then forgotten. The brain of the newborn contains practically all neurons but many are unconnected – learning is about creating connections between neurons and "maps" which, once consolidated, have important consequences for new learning. Learning for *a rapidly-changing world* can be understood through the acquisition of "meta-cognitive basic competencies" but neuroscience promises to give more precise understanding of the mechanisms involved and how practice-oriented learning takes place. *Emotions* and learning is a relatively new subject where neuroscience has insights to offer, especially the impact of negative emotions (fear, anxiety) on the ways in which learning takes place. Spitze outlines the relative role played by the hippocampus and the amygdala under different emotional states and how this can affect the learning process. He also discusses *the life cycle* and slowing rates of learning (seen as something positive, even necessary), brain plasticity throughout the lifespan, and the ways in which experience and judgement improve with age.

The "personal" domain as a social construct – changing conceptions of childhood and youth

---

Yvonne Hébert and William J. Hartley take the example of Canada for changes which occur through societies, shaped by moral, socio-economic, political and legal influences. These include the appearance of a more liberal Christianity, the growth of industrial and agricultural productivity, the spread of literacy and the rise of the middle class, the greater emancipation of women, and enlarged notions of citizenship. Two particular processes – the advent of mass schooling and the post-war development of teenage youth culture in advertising and through the media – have been instrumental in extending childhood and shaping youth. Among the different conceptions of childhood, one that runs through Canada's history is the notion of children and youth as consumers, producers, and commodities.

These sociological and historical perspectives are important in relation to the personalisation agenda. What counts as "personal" is not fixed but highly bound by cultural and historical factors. The possibilities to promote this agenda likewise are clearly influenced by such factors, and indeed they help to explain why this is emerging in some countries now as a policy priority. At the same time, educators are called upon to see beyond broad social representations of children and youth so as to support their strengths, legitimacy, diversity and vitality. Hence, there is need for sociological awareness while avoiding stereotypical images. Educational policy makers and researchers have a responsibility to understand conceptions of children and youth and to recognise the forces that shape them and young people must be recognised as whole.

Personalised learning in the broader
social picture

Jean-Claude Ruano-Borbalan traces the history of ideas and knowledge about learning to discuss the issue of personalisation with particular reference to France. An original characteristic of recent centuries, he argues, has been the development of massive systems to codify and reproduce society and a marked feature of such systems has been the form of their schools, classes and lessons. This is "efficient" when it comes to social reproduction and socialisation into society's values but not in terms of knowledge acquisition, learning capacity, and autonomy. Hence, however convincing the case for personalisation may be from the viewpoint of learning and the individual, we need to recognise the extent to which it may conflict with profound, longstanding social process. It also runs up against the strength of beliefs held especially by teachers about traditional modes of knowledge transmission. Ruano-Borbalan believes that the progressive element of the personalisation agenda is less in evidence in France now than it was 20-30 years ago.

Nevertheless, he proposes that we are at a "second modernity", borrowing a term from Giddens, with a gap between the dominant form of authority and knowledge transmission in the school system, on the one hand, and the scope for individuals to act and reflect, on the other. For modern societies, co-operation, networking and personalised learning are essential to economic and social development. Hence, the situation is one characterised by tensions. Because every human story is different, learning reflexes cannot be dictated and not by policy. But we can make a variety of activities and knowledge available to learners, in a range of educational situations and then let them decide "on their own", according to their preferences and personalities, how to progress and learn.

Prospects for personalised learning,
from now to 2025

Johan Peter Paludan from Denmark takes a futures orientation in this chapter to examine the elements that might lead the educational systems towards greater personalisation, namely, attitudes, motivation, the needs of society, and technological possibilities. In doing so, he warns against either underestimating the inertia of education systems or of overestimating their centrality for societies which now enjoy alternative routes to learning and knowledge. Nevertheless, lifelong learning itself presupposes a large degree of personalisation. Four scenarios are developed by combining two dimensions: economic growth (high to low) and culture (where the extremes are *laissez-faire* and tight control). This gives four scenarios: *1. total personalisation* (high growth and *laissez-faire*); *2. personalised timing* (high growth and tight control) *3. automated teaching* (low growth and *laissez faire*) 4. *the status quo* (low growth and tightening control). He assumes that personalised education will not be possible without simultaneously improving the productivity of the system, especially in circumstances of low growth.

The chapter considers how key stakeholders – students, teachers, parents, the labour market, society – might react. The analysis takes a frank view both of how personalisation might be positive for each stakeholder, and why each group might resist radical change in this direction. Moves towards personalisation may also mean that it becomes more difficult to ascertain what individual students have gained from their studies and more discontinuous education may have negative effects on society's cohesiveness. Personalisation characterised by easing the individual student's passage through the system will be much less controversial than one that also personalises educational content. A key theme developed by Paludan, despite his own conviction of the merits of moving in this broad direction, is that of resistance to change in situations where clarity of outcomes and stakeholder interests are challenged by the personalisation agenda.

The future of public services and
personalised learning

Charles Leadbeater argues that personalisation has the potential to reorganise the way public goods and services are created and delivered. It assumes that learners should be actively engaged in setting their own targets, devising their own learning plans and goals, choosing from among a range of different ways to learn. This chapter advances the discussion by exploring different concepts and approaches to personalisation, distinguishing between "shallow" and "deep" personalisation. The first is called *bespoke service*, where services are tailored to the needs of individual clients. The second approach outlined is called *mass customisation* in which users are allowed a degree of choice over how to mix and blend standard components to create learning programmes more suited to their goals. Third is *mass-personalisation*, based on participation and co-creation of value. Personalisation through participation allows users a more direct say in the way the service they use is designed, planned, delivered and evaluated. This involves the following steps: *intimate consultation, expanded choice, enhanced voice, partnership provision, advocacy, co-production*, and *funding*.

The context and the pressure for personalisation across a wide range of services is seen to be the chasm which has opened between people and large organisations, public and private. Hence, in education as in other sectors this agenda is seen as a way of reconnecting people to the institutions which serve them. As far as education is concerned, this implies far-reaching changes in the role of professionals and schools. But the biggest challenge is seen to be what it means for inequality: the more that services become personalised, the more that public resources will have to be skewed towards the least well-off.

Identifying the right questions about
personalisation of learning and public
services

Personalisation promises to overcome the uneven results of educational delivery and link innovation in the public sector to the broader transformations in OECD societies argue Tom Bentley and Riel Miller (at the time of the London conference of Demos and OECD respectively and its co-organisers). It is not purely a function of choice between alternative supply channels, but of shaping and combining different learning resources and sources of support around personal progression. Bentley and Miller discuss some familiar contrasts that can be re-cast by thorough-going personalisation. One is demand and supply, where the user (learner) may be directly involved in the design and creation of the learning experience. Another is public and private, where boundaries and the scope of each may be re-defined.

They describe entry points to system-wide change through different questions and issues. Universal? The first major challenge is to ensure that personalisation is not dominated by the already better-off. Diverse? At the moment subject diversity is the most prominent aspect of agendas, but as more dimensions are drawn in, what should these be? Transparent? This is about the role of data and information but which should these be and how far should they extend beyond the framework of existing institutions? There is the nature of learning, especially as we move away from the view of ability as something fixed and largely given towards a much more active, dynamic concept. They look at learning beyond the classroom and the role of communities. They consider the reshaping of roles in the educational workforce, and the way that personalisation might reshape the organisational patterns of schooling and related agencies. And, they consider how more responsive and adaptive organisational systems will be needed.

The system-wide shift that personalisation could help to stimulate, they conclude, has the potential to be as profound as any transition that public education systems have undertaken before, but this requires both a compelling political narrative and a strategy for distributed change.

Introduction

by
David Hopkins[*]

Personalising services is emerging as a key theme of policy across government and across the OECD. In one sense, personalisation represents a logical progression from the standards and accountability reform strategies that many countries implemented in the 1990s. They marked an important first phase in a long-term, large scale reform effort. But in order to sustain system-wide improvement, societies are increasingly demanding strategies characterised by diversity, flexibility and choice.

The imperative to personalise partly reflects the dynamic nature of people's aspirations; once they get the taste for learning, their appetite continues to grow, and we need school systems capable of stimulating and feeding that appetite. Within the OECD/CERI discussion, there has been a sustained focus on innovation and how to generate innovative capacity within school systems – that commitment to innovation is something which is now becoming part of the mainstream education debate – and is a vital element of the policy discussion.

Personalisation – from the political to the pedagogical

There is a huge amount we have to learn from each other and from the leading edge of practice in each system, and hence the value of this volume. But I would like to propose that the genesis of personalisation lies somewhere slightly different from the political emphasis with which it is currently associated. My argument is that the foundations of personalisation are partly historical, but mainly reflect an ethical root: it is *moral purpose* that drives personalisation.

---

[*] HSBC iNet Chair of International Leadership, Institute of Education, University of London, and former Chief Adviser to Ministers at the UK Department for Education and Skills (DfES), and former Director of the DfES Standards and Effectiveness Unit.

We see this moral purpose most vividly in the concern of the committed, conscientious teacher to match what is taught, and how it is taught, to the individual learner as a person. That is not just a question of "sufficient challenge" – of aligning pedagogy to the point of progression that each learner has reached, even though that is vitally important. It is part of the holistic nature of teaching as a profession, the concern to touch hearts as well as minds, to nourish a hunger for learning and help equip learners with a proficiency and confidence to pursue understanding for themselves. Emancipation is the heartland of personalisation. As Lawrence Stenhouse (1983) once said:

The essence of emancipation as I conceive it is the intellectual, moral and spiritual autonomy which we recognise when we eschew paternalism and the role of authority and hold ourselves obliged to appeal to judgement. (in *Authority, Education and Emancipation*, Heinemann Educational Books, London)

All teachers with a sense of vocation share this commitment, and virtually all attempt to differentiate how they teach to reflect the circumstances and the dispositions of the learners in front of them. But we also know that their efforts to do so are bounded by various factors:

- The limited extent to which schools can influence socio-economic variables which impact on learning.

- The limits of physical space, and the fact that teachers still have direct responsibility for whole groups of learners at any one time.

- The unsophisticated use of technology, whether print or computer, and the uniform pace of learning that they have traditionally demanded.

- The resiliently conservative nature of school organisation, and the step-by-step progression that virtually all children in every OECD system undertake.

- And crucially, the fact that teaching is still not an evidence-based profession and that the contingencies between learning and teaching are still not part of the day-to-day discourse of educators.

These frameworks and limitations have been everyday realities of schooling for decades. But, widespread innovation means we are in the process, as societies, of unlocking them. The challenge, therefore, is to connect the possibility of truly personalised pedagogy with the promise of more flexible, responsive, and transparent systems of organisation.

Achieving that combination is the challenge that this volume begins to address. I believe it makes an important contribution to sustaining reform, not only in the field of education, but through out the public sector. The broad reach of the diverse chapters, from a wide range of viewpoints and distinct national contexts, are the fruit of a conference held in London in 2004. Colleagues who played a key role in the conference and in pursuing the analysis of personalisation are acknowledged elsewhere in the introductions, but I especially want to underscore the important contribution made by David Miliband. He provides a clear message to policy makers regarding the centrality of personalisation for meeting tomorrow's public policy challenges. He also signals the need to reflect carefully on how to advance the personalisation agenda in light of international experience.

I believe that this volume makes contributions on both counts and constitutes a valuable point of reference in an ongoing discussion.

Chapter 1
Choice and Voice in Personalised Learning

by
David Miliband*

David Miliband, UK Schools Standards Minister at the time of the London personalisation conference, presents his vision and policy agenda for personalisation of learning. He outlines five components of personalised learning to guide policy development. i) It needs assessment for learning and the use of data and dialogue to diagnose every student's learning needs. ii) It calls for the development of the competence and confidence of each learner through teaching and learning strategies which build on individual needs. iii) It presupposes curriculum choice which engages and respects students. iv) It demands a radical approach to school organisation and class organisation based around student progress. v) Personalised learning means the community, local institutions and social services supporting schools to drive forward progress in the classroom. He develops the importance of the concepts of "choice" and "voice" as fundament to the personalisation agenda.

This conference comes at an absolutely key time for public services in Britain. I do not believe it is an exaggeration to say it is the most important time for public services since the creation of the welfare state after 1945. Now, as then, the power of collective action is being tested: to liberate individual potential, or to be damned for costing too much and delivering too little.

The Government fought the 2001 election on its commitment to public services. Since then, change has been consistent. Investment has never

---

* David Miliband, Member of Parliament is the UK Cabinet Minister of Communities and Local Government. He was the Schools Standards Minister at the time of the London 2004 Conference. This chapter is based on the speech he delivered at that conference.

grown faster; reform has never been more systematic; expectations have never been higher; and as the evidence has come in of rising quality in health, education and criminal justice systems, the prize of a public realm that promotes opportunity and security has rarely seemed closer. Yet the very enormity of effort means that the risks of failure, real or perceived, have never been greater. That is why those who believe that universal public service can never deliver have grown more shrill and more virulent in their denunciations of what is being done. They know we are at a key time – for our philosophy and theirs.

The politics and policy of this debate are intertwined. We should not shy away from that. Our focus today is policy; but the context is politics. Politics is not an intrusion into the debate about public services, but its necessary starting point. Politics itself should be a service to the public; and political debate frames the values, purpose, and shape of public services.

The social democratic settlement

The politics of the Government are simple: the social democratic settlement we seek aspires to make universal the life chances of the most fortunate. Collective services available on the basis of need, not ability to pay, are vital to that. In education, it means high standards of teaching available to all, shaped to individual need. Standing in the way are three great challenges: the challenge of equity and excellence; the challenge of flexibility and accountability; and the challenge of universality and personalisation.

We see the challenge of excellence and equity in many debates, from Foundation Hospitals to university funding to specialist schooling. In an unequal society, how can excellent provision serve the least fortunate, rather than the most? One answer is to say it cannot; excellence will always be monopolised by the well-off, so a social democratic approach should be simply to tackle poor performance.

I believe this is profoundly wrong. We must obviously tackle failure. But aside from the absurdity of trying to put a glass ceiling on the achievement of different services, excellence can be used as a battering ram against inequality. This is the experience of specialist schools and the Excellence in Cities and Leading Edge programmes in education. Excellence is a resource for a more egalitarian system, not a threat. It can do more than set an example; it can be a locomotive for improvement across the system.

The second challenge is how to combine flexibility in delivery with accountability for results. No one believes every community has the same needs; but flexibility on its own can lead to poverty of aspiration and paucity of provision. The answer must be intelligent accountability: a system that both supports improvement and challenges the lack of it. This requires central and local government to speak up for the fragmented voice of the consumer, and make good the market failure that allows underperformance to continue. It requires public information on performance that commands the confidence of professionals and citizens. It demands central intervention to set minimum standards, with intervention in inverse proportion to success. And, it requires funding to be delegated to the frontline as soon as capacity exists there, giving full flexibility to meet local need.

But the focus of this conference and my focus today is the third challenge: the demand that universal services have a personal focus. My interest, or at least my starting point, is personal. In the late 1980s, I was a graduate student in the United States, and was taught by Charles Sabel, co-author with Michael Piore of *The Second Industrial Divide* (1990). Its argument was simple: the era of mass production would be superseded in the advanced economies by the age of flexible specialisation, products previously produced for a mass market now to be tuned to personal need. That revolution, fuelled by rising affluence and expectations, has not been confined to the world of business. It has found its way into social norms through the end of deference; its manifestation in public services is the demand for high standards suited to individual need.

Until recently, the debate in the UK has been polarised into an argument between advocates of market solutions and those who favoured a planned approach. Our purpose in Government is to provide a new choice for those who are not satisfied to rely solely on the state or the market. In education we know that planned systems can be tolerant of under-performance – bureaucratic and inefficient. But we also know that in the 1990s nursery vouchers failed to stimulate supply and instead created chaos. Meanwhile we know parental choice in schools can be valuable in itself and a spur to parental engagement. But we also know it is a very slow way of putting pressure on underperforming schools to improve, and in any case few parents want to choose a school more than twice – one primary, one secondary – in a pupil's career.

So we need to do more than engage and empower pupils and parents in the selection of a school: their engagement has to be effective in the day-by-day processes of education. It should be at the heart of the way schools create partnerships with professional teachers and support staff to deliver tailor-made services. In other words, we need to embrace individual empowerment within as well as between schools. This leads straight to the promise of personalised learning. It means building the organisation of schooling around the needs, interests and aptitudes of individual pupils; it means shaping teaching around the way different youngsters learn; it means taking the care to nurture the unique talents of every pupil. I believe it is *the* debate in education today.

The five components of personalised learning

Personalised learning is not a return to child-centred theories; it is not about separating pupils to learn on their own; it is not the abandonment of a national curriculum; and it is not a license to let pupils coast at their own preferred pace of learning. The rationale for personalised learning is clear: it is to raise standards by focusing teaching and learning on the aptitudes and interests of pupils. Personalised learning is the way in which our best schools tailor education to ensure that every pupil achieves the highest standard possible. Our drive is to make these best practices universal. There are five key elements to doing so.

First, a personalised offer in education depends on really knowing the strengths and weaknesses of individual students. So, the biggest driver for change is *assessment for learning and the use of data and dialogue* to diagnose every student's learning needs.

We know from the Office for Standards in Education (Ofsted, responsible for the inspection of schools in England), the power of assessment for learning to provide structured feedback to pupils, to set individual learning targets, and to help plan lessons according to individual needs. Ofsted tells us that just four out of ten secondary schools use assessment for learning well, so we know there is still much to do. Embed these practices in all schools and we will achieve a step-change in achievement. That is why the Pupil Achievement Tracker[1] is now at the heart of our drive to ensure critical self review of performance in every school.

Second, personalised learning demands that we develop the competence and confidence of each learner through *teaching and learning strategies that build on individual needs*. This requires strategies that actively engage and stretch all students, that creatively deploy teachers, support staff and new technologies to extend learning opportunities, and that accommodate different paces and styles of learning.

This is not a crude reductionism to specific learner "types". It is recognition that the multiple intelligences of pupils require a repertoire of teaching strategies. It is also about students acquiring the skills to fulfil their

---

[1] The Pupil Achievement Tracker (PAT) software allows schools and Local Education Authorities (LEAs) to import and analyse their own pupil performance data against national performance data.

own potential, by ensuring that they have the capability and accept the responsibility to take forward their own learning. This is something that impressed me on a visit to George Spencer Technology College in Nottingham, where I saw students attending learning-to-learn lessons to help them become effective and e-literate learners – on their own and in groups.

Third, *curriculum choice engages and respects students*. So, personalised learning means every student enjoying curriculum choice, a breadth of study and personal relevance, with clear pathways through the system. In primary schools, it means students gaining high standards in the basics allied to opportunities for enrichment and creativity. In the early secondary years, it means students actively engaged by exciting curricula, problem solving, and class participation. And then at 14-19, it means significant curriculum choice for the learner.

This is the importance of the Tomlinson working group on 14-19 education,[2] with the long-term goals for all students of stretch, incentives to learn, core skills and specialist vocational and academic options. It is a future already being charted by diverse groups of schools, colleges and employers across the country, for instance, in the Central Gateshead 6th Form which offers a common prospectus, a wide range of academic and vocational courses, and a choice of movement for students across participating institutions. There is a group of schools in Nottingham that is working with local media companies to provide students with a multi-media programme that combines in-school delivery with real life experience of the industry.

Fourth, personalised learning demands *a radical approach to school organisation*. It means the starting point for class organisation is always student progress, with opportunities for in-depth, intensive teaching and learning, combined with flexible deployment of support staff. Workforce reform is a key factor. The real professionalism of teachers can best be developed when they have a range of adults working at their direction to meet diverse student needs. It also means guaranteed standards for on-site services, such as catering and social areas. Only if we offer the best to pupils will we get the best. And it means a school ethos focused on student needs, with the whole school team taking time to find out the needs and interests of students; with students listened to and their voice used to drive whole school improvement; and with the leadership team providing a clear focus for the progress and achievement of every child.

---

[2] The Working Group on 14-19 Reform, chaired by Mike Tomlinson, was established in Spring 2003 and following consultation with a wide variety of partners and stakeholders, published its Final Report, "14-19 Curriculum and Qualifications Reform", also known as the Tomlinson Report, on 18 October 2004.

Fifth, personalised learning means the *community, local institutions and social services supporting schools* to drive forward progress in the classroom. There is already real innovation:

- At Grange Primary School in Long Eaton, the building of a stronger partnership with parents through regular communication about each child's progress, so that parents gain the confidence and knowledge to provide effective support at home.

- At Millfields Community school in Hackney some of the effect of creative thinking about how best to support learning beyond the school day – by offering students a breakfast club, an after-school club and a Saturday school that teaches an accelerated learning curriculum – can be seen in the outstanding improvement in attainment at age 11.

- In different areas of the country, Creative Partnerships are bringing together schools and local artists and creative institutions in a systematic and structured relationship to enrich the educational offer through the expertise of professionals without teaching qualifications but with real ability to contribute to the learning experience of young people. The same is happening in the more than 100 museums and galleries working systematically to raise achievement and enjoyment.

- Across the country, schools and Local Education Authorities (LEAs) are anticipating the demands of the current Children's Bill, trying to ensure that the most vulnerable young people have integrated support from a range of professionals, all dedicated to supporting educational achievement as the best hope for the future of the child.

So, there are five components of personalised learning. They are a challenge to Government, to schools, and to the wider community. But they are massively in the interests of pupils.

There is then the question of how to see them developed. The demand is there: parents want education that is right for their children. Open enrolment and specialisation broaden the scope for parents to express a preference for a school that they think suits their child's needs. But the model of consumer choice is insufficient – not irrelevant but insufficient – to make it happen. The challenge is to ally choice with voice: voice for the pupil, voice for the parent. That is the new frontier for education. Personalised learning aims to engage every parent and every child in the educational experience.

Choice and voice

Over thirty years ago, the American sociologist Albert Hirschman published his classic study *Exit, Voice and Loyalty: Responses to Decline in*

Firms, Organizations and States. His opening comment – that the book "has its origin in an observation on rail transportation in Nigeria" – may seem a far cry from personalised learning. But the book has a key lesson for the debate about how to raise quality in public services. Hirschman's argument is simple: that while competition and customer exit are vital to the process of economic renewal and progress, "a major alternative mechanism can come into play either when the competitive mechanism is unavailable or as a complement to it".

That mechanism is consumer voice. For Hirschman, voice is the attempt to change from within, rather than escape, a particular institution – be it a shop or a school. Its traditional association is with the world of politics rather than economics. And its association in politics is with argument and debate in political parties and voluntary organisations. It assumes collective deliberation, usually in draughty halls or smoke-filled rooms.

The magic of Hirschman's book is two-fold. First, its simple proposition is that the dichotomy of choice and voice is a false one. The market sphere offers voice as well as choice, the political sphere choice as well as debate. Second, the arresting idea that choice and voice are strengthened by the presence of the other: the threat of exit makes companies and parties listen; the ability to make your voice heard provides a vital tool to the consumers who do not want to change shops, or political parties, every time they are unhappy.

A key difference in public services is that supply is limited – for example places at a school. Education needs drive the supply side and government has a responsibility to stimulate it. But personalised learning also needs an active demand side – and that means voice as well as choice. We can and must combine the empowerment of parents and pupils in choices about schools and courses and activities with their genuine engagement in the search for higher standards. This is exemplified in our efforts to develop a personalised offer for a particular group of pupils – those in the top 5-10% of the ability range who are the gifted and talented.

Gifted and talented provision

Bright students have too often been confronted by the very British mentality which says it's wrong to celebrate success and worse still to actively encourage it. The bright student was too often embarrassed by being labelled a "smart-Alec"; the result was at best day-dreaming, at worst frustration leading to trouble. The dominant culture fell into the trap of believing that "ordinary" children did not have extraordinary talents. There was no vocabulary, never mind systematic tailored provision, to advance the case. This is a clear case of personalised learning being sadly absent.

Recently, there has been a step change. We are getting better at celebrating success; better at challenging a culture of low aspirations; better at responding to the unique needs of our brightest students. And vitally, we are doing so by focusing our support in our most disadvantaged areas, because whilst potential is not linked to class, the support and opportunities needed for it to thrive too often have been.

- Schools in our toughest areas had the least provision. That is why the Excellence in Cities programme[3] has a strand devoted to Gifted and Talented provision. It now reaches over 150 000 students in 2 000 public primary and 1 000 public secondary schools.

- Provision did not sufficiently develop the learning capacity of bright students. That is why we now expect there to be a trained Gifted and Talented co-ordinator in every participating school, ensuring that the top 5-10% are identified by ability, and that they receive a tailored teaching and learning programme and complementary out-of-school study support.

- Provision in London was particularly weak. That is why we have introduced London Gifted and Talented as part of the London Challenge (a policy partnership programme to address the problems and challenges faced by education and young people in the capital). London's strength depends more than ever on its education system: it needs to develop a coherent regional approach across all 33 London boroughs built on bottom-up collaboration and an innovatory e-learning platform that benefits pupils and teachers alike.

- National leadership was absent. That is why we set up the National Academy for Gifted and Talented Youth at Warwick University, which now delivers summer schools, e-learning provision and learning networks to the 28 000 members of its Student Academy.

- Teachers were under-engaged. That is why the professional arm of the National Academy brings support staff, teachers and head teachers together to collaborate on best practice in the teaching and learning of gifted and talented students, and to use these strategies to improve provision for all students; it is why we are developing quality standards for classroom teachers; and it is why Ofsted now takes gifted and talented provision seriously in their inspections.

---

[3] Excellence in Cities (EiC) is a targeted UK government programme of support for schools in deprived areas of the country.

We have started to break down old divides, and unleashed talent which in previous years would have been hidden forever. But we have only started. I want to ensure all gifted and talented students gain from personalised learning. The goal is that five years from now:

- Gifted and talent students progress in line with their ability rather than their age.

- Schools inform parents about tailored provision in an annual school profile.

- Curricula include a gifted and talented dimension, and at age 14-19 there is more stretch and differentiation at the top end, so no matter what your talent it will be engaged.

- The effect of poverty on achievement is reduced, because support for high-ability students from poorer backgrounds enables them to thrive at school and progress to our leading universities.

In five years' time, the impact of gifted and talented provision should be as important for school pupils in widening opportunities, removing barriers to excellence, and putting learners in control as the establishment of the Open University in the late 1960s was to university students – as radical in its conception, as wide in its reach. It should be a future in which society is based on talent, not held back by an old boys' network based on who you know; a future in which students do better because education is tailored to their needs.

And what is the moral of the story? First, that fragmented demand will not always produce coherent supply. Second, we have to trust pupils to make choices, but also recognise that we must listen to them as well as empower them. Every member of the Student Academy chooses courses and activities that they prefer. Those that are not attractive will not thrive. But we do best when we listen to student voice in the creation of student choice. That is what the National Academy is doing in its programmes for the gifted and talented, and although perhaps the more challenging task is listening to the average student less certain about their needs, that is what an increasing numbers of schools are doing in their Student Councils.

Conclusion

The Welsh Labour politician Aneurin Bevan used to say that the freedom to choose was worthless without the power to choose. This is the power of personalised learning. Not a false dichotomy between choice and voice but acceptance that if we are to truly revolutionise public services then people need to have both. Because students are not merely educational shoppers in the marketplace; they are creators of their own educational experience. Their voice can help shape provision, both as a means of engaging students in their own learning – the co-producers of education – and as a means of developing their talents – using their voice to help create choices.

We want to take this programme forward. We need to develop and communicate the benefits of personalised learning. Our greatest resource is in our schools but national dialogue, as in this conference, can help. There are two key strands. We need to develop a common language and clarity of concepts among professionals. But we must also listen to pupils. The new frontier in business is not flexible specialisation but personal experience. We must not get left behind.

The prize is immense: an education system based on need, an education system where choice is available for the many not the few; an education system where the system is moulded around the child, not the child around the system; an education system that identifies the true potential of every child and then gives them the means to achieve it. It is what every parent wants for their child, and as the eminent historian and social critic R.H. Tawney said, it should be what Government wants for every child.

References

Hirschman, A. (1970), *Exit, Voice and Loyalty: Responses to Decline in Firms, Organizations and States*, Harvard University Press, United States.

Sabel, C. and M. Piore (1990), *The Second Industrial Divide: Possibilities for Prosperity*, Basic Books, United States.

Chapter 2
Personalised Learning?
New Insights into Fostering Learning Capacity

by
Sanna Järvelä*

Sanna Järvelä reviews research evidence and clarified key questions relating to personalisation. She concludes that personalisation of learning has become imperative. By this, she does not mean individualised learning nor the opposite of social learning but as an approach in educational policy and practice whereby every student matters, equalising opportunities through learning skills and motivation to learn. She examines seven critical dimensions: i) development of key skills which are often domain-specific; ii) levelling the educational playing field through guidance for improvement of students' learning skills and motivation; iii) encouragement of learning through "motivational scaffolding"; iv) collaboration in knowledge-building; v) development of new models of assessment; vi) use of technology as a personal cognitive and social tool; vii) the new role of teachers in better integration of education within the learning society.

The rapidly changing educational, vocational and leisure activities of modern society present lifelong adaptive challenges for humankind. From early childhood, individuals encounter masses of complex, symbolic information and diverse cultural products. They are also constantly called upon to renew their social relations, forcing them to confront considerable novelty and ambiguity. Such environments place a heavy burden on the individual's adaptive capacity and resources. Learning is at the core of this process.

Successfully meeting the learning challenges of today's knowledge- and competence-oriented society demands disciplined study and problem

* Professor of Education and the head of the Research Unit for Educational Technology in the Faculty of Education at the University of Oulu, Finland.

solving from the earliest years. At work, there is continuous need to improve quality, creativity and performance in knowledge-intensive settings. In the home and community, people face a wide range of choices that can only be effectively resolved through learning. At the same time, new information and communication technologies are generating more open and flexible ways of learning.

In this general context, personalised learning is a potential approach to meeting future educational needs and may provide new alternatives that foster learning capacity among individual learners (Bentley and Miller, 2004). However, when thinking about personalising learning, care must be taken to remain realistic in terms of the individual's ability to be a competent, adaptive, active, goal-oriented and motivated learner. It is also important to take into account the scope of the social and collaborative processes of learning communities. This chapter investigates the power of personalised learning systems along seven critical dimensions:

- Development of key skills which are often domain-specific.

- Levelling the educational playing field through guidance for improvement of students' learning skills and motivation.

- Encouragement of learning through a "motivational scaffolding".

- Collaboration in knowledge-building.

- Development of new models of assessment.

- Use of technology as a personal cognitive and social tool.

- Teachers' new role in better integration of education within the learning society.

Development of key skills

What kind of knowledge will future learning and work situations require? To what extent should domain-specific competencies be personalised? Depending on the characteristics of the learning domains, some tasks and environments support individual work, while others will support a community of learners working on the same task. Mastering the characteristics of these tasks requires a sound knowledge base that must be constructed in light of the tasks and the competencies of the pertinent field of knowledge.

Recent advancements in social-focused analyses of learning have complemented individual-focused studies of human learning (Anderson *et al.*, 2000). Overall the results highlight the social construction of knowledge and the control processes involved in learning partnerships, particularly when it comes to shared cognition and regulation. In light of these studies, it has become clear that education systems need to consider the development of personalised expertise and the skills needed to build distributed expertise.

Knowledge construction and knowledge sharing form the core processes of learning. Both of these processes need to be connected to the development of higher order knowledge and skills, which should be seen as key organisers for how and what kinds of knowledge become relevant and shared. Higher order skills are understood here as the ability to evaluate, classify, make inferences, define problems and reflect (Brandsford and Stein, 1993). This implies the ability to sort out facts, conceptual arguments and assumptions embedded in the presented information and knowledge. Reading and producing text, models, graphs and multimedia in different genres are key elements in the development of advanced knowledge that require higher order skills (Brown, 1997). Higher order skills need to be perceived both as skills people have developed through their practical activities, and as skills that must be developed in order to master different types of practices. Both of these skills must be acquired to respond to the learning challenges of humankind. Through personalised learning, students are taught to use conceptual and factual knowledge in purposeful activities in authentic environments.

Levelling the playing field

Analytical skills, thinking skills, and learning strategies should be taught in schools. Teaching analytical thinking means encouraging students to analyse, critique, judge, compare and contrast, evaluate and assess – but also to continue creative and practical thinking.

Researchers agree that frequent and deliberate use of learning strategies is related to academic achievement (Boekarts, Pintrich and Zeidner, 2000). Earlier studies have shown that a selection of appropriate strategies can empower learning. Strategic learners have the following qualities: they are better aware of themselves as learners, they employ different knowledge acquisition strategies, they understand the specifics of task qualifications, they connect prior knowledge content to new knowledge and the possible contexts where knowledge could be useful, and they engage in meta-cognitive activities while learning.

In addition to the development of thinking skills, Sternberg (2003) has proposed going beyond conventional notions of expertise and strategic learning in order to teach children not only to think well, but also wisely. His approach differs from conventional teaching, which emphasises the development of an expert knowledge base primarily through the application of memory and analytical skills. His theory of successful intelligence (Sternberg and Grigorenko, 2000) extends the basis of developing expertise by integrating teaching for creative and practical skills with teaching for strategic learning. It should be noted, nevertheless, that students can become content experts without using their expertise in the search for a common good. An augmented conception of expertise might also take into account the extent to which knowledge is put to wise and intelligent use for collective well-being.

Motivating learners

Humans have the capacity to learn throughout their lives in diverse contexts. Students should be provided with "motivated learning schemas" and equal opportunities to work in different learning environments, thus enabling them to participate in the type of learning activities that promote learning and understanding (Volet and Järvelä, 2001).

Traditionally, school learning has trained students to achieve explicitly delineated goals. Emphasis can be placed on other types of learning situations that teach students to appreciate the value of what they are doing and learning. Furthermore, learning situations might be developed that involve lifelong learning, or, at the very least, sustained engagement in particular interest areas that often lead to the development of expertise (Brophy, 1999). Personalised learning can increase the value of learning. How learners may come to value particular learning domains or activities, and how teachers or parents might stimulate the development of such values are two core issues that must be explained. Motivationally effective teachers make school learning experiences meaningful for students in two fundamental ways: cognitively, by enabling students to learn and understand content, and motivationally, by allowing them to appreciate its value, particularly its potential applications in their lives outside of school.

When developing a personalised learning approach, the focus should be not only on how to strengthen students' self-regulation skills (*e.g.* set learning goals and train students to achieve them), but also how to show them the value of learning in order to understand. A broader question is: how can people be motivated to build up competence and anticipate future needs both in local communities and in society at large in order to prevent segregation and exclusion?

Collaborative knowledge-building

One of the essential requirements in the rapidly changing society is to prepare learners to participate in socially organised activities. A pure focus on individual cognition may set the stage for a shared, interactive and social construction of knowledge. It is crucial to recognise that new learning environments in school and the work-place are often based on collaborative and shared expertise. These environments work under the presumption that learners are capable to work as team members and share their opinions and ideas.

Collaborative learning and knowledge building is one of the most meaningful ways to support individual learning mechanisms (Bereiter and Scardamalia, 1989). Studies of collaborative learning (Dillenbourg, 1999) have shown that it is effective if the students engage in rich interactions. Through this process learners arrive at complex and conceptual understanding rather than simple answers. This leads to the question: how could the collaborative process in personalised learning be regulated in order to favour the emergence of these types of interactions? For example, how can technology be designed to enhance personalised learning environments in ways that increase the possibility that such rich interactions occur?

New pedagogical models, tools and practices that support collaborative learning are being developed as a response to the increased need for sharing and constructing new perspectives, exploiting distributed expertise and increasing reciprocal understanding. Recently, educational researchers have worked towards developing pedagogical models for collaborative learning, such as inquiry approaches or problem-based learning. Research results show that these kinds of learning models generally indicate that inquiry learning fosters productive task-related interaction and enhances student motivation in general (Blumenfeld *et al.*, 1991; Hakkarainen, Lipponen and Järvelä, 2002). Other studies of student learning in computer supported environments that apply socio-constructivist pedagogical models report similar findings on more enduing adaptive tendencies (Cognition and Technology Group at Vanderbild, 1992; Hickey, Moore and Pellegrino, 2001).

However, it is crucial to note that there are also variations in the quality of the learning processes among students: some students have major difficulties in engaging in research-like working procedures with technology, and their learning processes may be more regressive than progressive (Krajcik *et al.*, 1998; Veermans and Järvelä, 2004). Even though the learning results seem promising, more research and implementation of these learning models are needed. A few examples of these pedagogical models – progressive inquiry, problem-based and project-based – help clarify the need both for further research and the implications for personalised learning.

Progressive inquiry

The instructional design of progressive inquiry promotes processes of advancing and constructing knowledge, which are characteristic of scientific inquiry. It guides students to generate their own research problems and intuitive theories and to search for explanatory information (Hakkarainen and Sintonen, 2002). Participating students share all elements of inquiry in order to foster their understanding.

A process of inquiry can be divided into different phases, each of which has its own specific objective and function in the process. Accordingly, every phase has a special dimension from the motivational point of view. The starting point of the process of inquiry is creating context for a study project in order to help students understand why the issues in question are important and worthwhile. They then become personally committed to solving the problems under investigation. This phase should arouse intrinsic motivation and understanding of the value of learning (Brophy, 1999). An essential aspect of inquiry is to set up questions or problems that guide the process of inquiry. Questions that arise from the students' own need to understand have a special value. Further, the questions should be in explanation-seeking rather than fact-oriented form in order to direct the process towards deeper understanding (Scardamalia and Bereiter, 1994). By creating a working theory of their own, students can systematically use their background knowledge and make inferences to extend their understanding. This phase enables students to be more involved in the process, because they can feel that they are contributors to knowledge (Cognition and Technology Group at Vanderbilt, 1992). The phase of searching and sharing new information helps students to become aware of their inadequate presuppositions or background information. This phase requires students to comment on each other's notes and encourages collaboration (Dillenbourg, 1999). A critical condition for progress is that students focus on improving their theory by generating and setting up subordinate questions. These questions will lead students towards deepening the process of inquiry (Hakkarainen and Sintonen, 2002).

Problem-based learning (PBL)

This learning method is a collaborative, case-centred, and learner-directed method of instruction, where problem formulation, knowledge application, self-directed learning, abstraction and reflection are seen as essential components (Koschmann *et al.*, 1996). These components arise from constructivist propositions, which can also be seen as instructional principles: all learning activities should be anchored to a larger task or problem, the learner should be engaged in scientific activities which present the same "type" of cognitive challenges as an authentic learning environment, and the learning environment should support and challenge the learner's thinking (Savery and Duffy, 1996). The learning environment of PBL and the task should be designed in a way that they reflect the complexity of the environment. When conducting inquiry around a task, the learner should be given ownership of the process she or he uses to develop a solution. Teachers still have a role in guiding the process. They ensure, for example, that a particular problem solving or critical thinking methodology will be used or that particular content domains will be "learned". As in other collaborative learning methods, PBL students are encouraged to test their ideas against alternative views and within alternative contexts.

There are many strategies for implementing PBL, but usually the general scenario is the same (Barrows, 1986; Savery and Duffy, 1996). The students are divided into groups of four to five, and each group has a facilitator. Then these groups are presented a problem that they are supposed to study and solve. Based on the knowledge the students have, they try to generate hypothesis of the problem by discussing with each other. After clarifying the problem, the students engage in self-directed learning to gather information from many different sources. After this individual studying phase, the students meet again in their groups. They evaluate the information they found to gather the essential pieces needed to solve the problem. This social negotiation of meaning is an important part of the learning process. The students begin to work on the problem and again, re-conceptualise their problem to more specific sub-problems. At the end of the process usually peer- and self-evaluation is used. This kind of PBL cycle takes some time, for example, in medical education it takes from one to three weeks to conduct the PBL cycle.

Project-based learning

Project-based learning can be seen as a way to promote high-level learning by engaging students in real scientific work. They learn by undertaking complex, challenging and authentic projects. To carry out the constructivist theory of learning, the main aim is that students actively construct knowledge by working with and using ideas (Blumenfeld *et al.*, 1991). In a project, students engage in a complex process of inquiry and design. The result is an artefact, based on the students' knowledge, which can be critiqued and shared. The public display of the artefact can motivate student involvement. The risk of this kind of project is that it results in a focus on task-completion. Often in such projects, the final artefact is central rather than the knowledge produced during the course of its creation. For example, if students make a poster; there is emphasis on task-completion.

At the same time, as students are choosing the topic of their project, they are also studying many skills and forms of knowledge that are tacit or deeply embedded within a practice. It has been argued that in this model of collaborative learning, the projects provide the best opportunity for students to understand these embedded or non-decomposable skills and knowledge (Guzdial, 1998). In the past, project-based learning has been used with science subject matters. Writing specifically about science learning, Krajcik *et al.* (1998) proposed some features the learning process should include:

- A driving question, encompassing worthwhile content.

- Investigations that allow students to ask and refine questions.

- Artefacts that allow students to learn concepts.

- Collaboration among students, teachers, and others in the learning community.

- Technology that supports student data-gathering, analysis, communicating and document preparation.

To sum up, project-based learning environments encourage learning by doing and are crucial to personalised learning. These environments create opportunities for students to explore and solve world problems in the classroom. Content and process become inseparable during the discovery and inquiry phase of learning. Thus students remain constantly engaged in the investigation of the problem. They identify gaps in their knowledge, search for and analyse the information needed to solve problems, and develop their own solutions. This approach to learning differs greatly from "typical" school classrooms in which students spend most of their time listening to lectures, or learning facts from texts and completing problems in the end of a textbook chapter.

New methods of assessment

The core questions dealing with assessment in personalised learning environments are:

- What do learners understand about their studies?

- How can learners generate information about how much they have learned and how their knowledge is changing?

- What should be evaluated?

- What is the relation between formal and non-formal education in terms of assessment?

Personalised learning requires new modes of assessment, such as authentic assessment, performance assessment, or (digital) portfolios. By expanding the range of abilities measured and ways of making the measurements, other intellectual strengths that might not have been apparent through conventional testing can be found and students' own self-beliefs of learning strengthened.

Effective teachers see assessment opportunities in ongoing classroom learning situations. They continually attempt to learn about students' thinking and understanding and make it relevant for current tasks. They do a great deal of on-line monitoring of both group work and individual performance, and attempt to link current activities to other parts of the curriculum and to student daily life experiences (Brandsford, Brown and Cocking, 2000).

Finding new methods of assessment becomes essential when information and communication technology play more central roles in studying and learning (Sinko and Lehtinen, 1999). Conventional standardised measurements for assessing learning are not always relevant when students are working with technology-based learning environments. For example, it is not possible to measure on the individual level the way that students work as a team to create new knowledge and solve joint problems. New methods need to be developed to measure, for example, how a student's capacity to participate in the activities has increased or how his inquiry-making has changed.

Using technology

How can technology be used to advance personalised learning needs in different life-wide contexts? How can collaborative learning activities be developed in different learning environments, including virtual ones? For personalised learning to succeed, it will be important to develop models that use technology to support individual and social learning activities. Multidisciplinary collaboration between technology developers and educational designers need to find ways to apply virtual spaces, simulations, game-technology or mobile applications to learning.

Many European countries have made efforts to use information and communication technology (ICT) in education. For example, the Finnish strategy says: "In developing the use of information and communication technologies in education, the objective is to shift the focus from hardware to pedagogic renewal and help increasing numbers of pupils to learn increasingly demanding information structures and problem-solving skills. In education, the emphasis lies on high-quality contact education, communality, interaction, open and flexible expression, and the use of distributed expertise through networks." (Information Strategy for Education and Research 2000-2004, Ministry of Education in Finland)

The core message of this strategy is that our rapidly changing society necessitates new forms of participation. Modern working environments involving intensive collaboration, expertise sharing, and social knowledge construction are permanent, and therefore contribute to setting new norms for educational standards. The pressure to develop responsive pedagogical practices is evident. Within this quest, pedagogical approaches that seek to utilise advanced technical infrastructures to foster higher-level processes of inquiry-based interaction have been considered most plausible (Strijbos, Kirschner and Martens, 2004; Wasson, Ludvigsen and Hoppe, 2003). By combining the ideas of collaborative learning and networked technology, these approaches aim at turning classrooms of students into communities of learners and learning situations into challenging and interesting projects with authentic problems. Such inquiry activities provide a valuable context for learners to acquire, clarify, and apply an understanding of concepts in different domains.

Based on research and practical experience, the following principles are the best arguments for implementing ICT in learning:

- ICT can increase authenticity and interest.

- ICT can build virtual communities among different schools, collaborating teams, and teachers.

- ICT can help to share perspectives among students with different expertise; proving peer support and "benchmarking practices" in different fields.

- ICT facilitates the use of technology-supported inquiry approaches and problem-based models for increasing learning-to-learn skills.

- ICT provides innovative ways (for example, mobile tools) of integrating "just-in-time" support and interaction in different learning contexts.

One of the trends of the future will be the use of mobile devices and wireless networks for education. Mobile phone use is widespread today, and, increasingly, students and young people also use handheld computers and other mobile devices. This leads us to conclude that the pedagogical use of wireless devices will be one future challenge. Roschelle and Pea (2002) suggest that future classrooms are likely to be organised around Wireless Internet Learning Devices (WILD) that resemble graphing calculators or

Palm handhelds, connected by short-range wireless networking. WILD learning will have physical advantages that are different from today's computer lab or classrooms with many students sharing a single computer. According to Roschelle and Pea, these differing advantages may lead to learning activities that deviate significantly from today's images for computer- and technology-based learning activities. The main reason for the pedagogical use of mobile devices is a) to enhance collaborative learning through cognitive interaction using mobile applications and cultural artefacts; and b) interaction among the student both inside and outside of the schools and classrooms as well as knowledge building communities.

In spite of record development of technology, recent evaluative studies of the role of information and communication technology in teaching and learning (*e.g.* Hakkarainen, Lipponen and Järvelä, 2002; Niemivirta and Järvelä, 2003; Khaili and Shashaani, 1994) do not show significantly better results for technology versus non-technology mediated learning. However, there seems to be considerable payoff from the indirect impact of using ICT on part of the overall learning environment. First, enriching schools, classrooms, and offices with technology has made teachers and students change old habits and create more innovative pedagogical models. Second, the prevalence of Internet access, wireless networks, and virtual universities and schools has led to an increased collaboration among teachers, students, and administrators. Third, the results of the longitudinal empirical studies as well as case studies in different computer-enriched learning projects tell us that ICT is particularly effective for lifelong learning because it facilitates progressive motivational experiences and more advanced study strategies among the students.

There has been a systematic effort by the European Union and individual nations to implement educational use of ICTs. However, there are still many challenges to overcome if learning- and education-use of ICT is not accessible to the majority (Lehtinen, Sinko and Hakkarainen, 2001). Issues such as a shortage of high-quality digital learning materials and insufficient pedagogical and technical support are still very real. Furthermore, teacher training needs to be improved and better focused. Also, a sufficient level of research and development of high-level learning environments must be sustained in order to improve the implementation of promising practices. Personalised learning offers a potential framework to further develop these practices in pedagogical development and educational policy.

New roles for teachers

Teachers and trainers are likely to encounter transitional problems when implementing personalised learning that are parallel to those of learners as they move from conventional to new, open, and less-structured learning environments. New learning environments require complex instructional design. Teachers will need to reconsider communication and collaboration skills. They will have to develop new pedagogical reflective thinking in mentoring learning, mediating values and social skills, as well as systematically evaluating students' and teacher's own activities. What is the teacher's role and expertise as mentor in collaborative- and socially-shared learning? What kind of new teacher training contents, models and methods can be used for implementing learning innovations? How should teachers be encouraged to create a new teaching and learning culture in schools and in open learning environments? How should the growth of teachers as lifelong learners be supported in the future? How can teachers facilitate partnerships for promoting life-wide learning in a civil society?

Teachers are key to personalised learning. In order to teach in a manner consistent with new theories of learning, teachers require their own extensive learning opportunities. What is known about learning applies to teachers as much as to their students. Research evidence indicates that the most successful professional development activities for teachers are those that are extended over time and encourage the development of teachers' learning communities (Brandsford, Brown and Cocking, 2000). These kinds of activities are accomplished by creating opportunities for shared expertise and discourse around shared texts and data about student learning and by focussing on shared decision making. Teachers' learning communities also allow for different backgrounds and variations in readiness to learn.

Conclusion

To sum up, the main arguments from the point of view of learning theory for personalising learning and fostering learning capacities are:

- Personalising learning can improve conditions for the development of expertise in the knowledge society. Collaborative efforts and networked forms of expertise are increasingly needed in the future knowledge society.

- Personalising learning increases student interest and engagement in learning activities. If students are able to develop their personal learning and individual expertise in the areas in which they either feel incompetent or in need to increase their existing expertise then their individual interest in learning can be enhanced. Curiosity and creativity can be inspired by personalised learning.

- Personalising learning can contribute to better learning results if students learn with the aim of developing: develop better learning strategies, learning to learn skills, technological capacities for individual and social learning activities, and create learning communities with collaborative learning models.

- Personalising learning can take contextual conditions into account. There is a variety of learning contexts in European countries, from urban areas to rural and remote areas. Different values and cultural features can be respected if the individual person and his/her needs are deemed important.

- Personalising learning can potentially improve the use of technology in education. When technology is seen as an intelligent tool for supporting individual learning as well as collaborative learning among different individuals there are multiple ways to expand learning potential in every student.

Personalisation of learning has become imperative. This does not mean that purely individualised learning, nor is it the opposite of social learning. Personalised learning can be seen as an approach in educational policy and practice whereby every student matters. It equalises learning opportunities in terms of learning skills and motivation to learn.

References

Anderson, J.R., J.G. Greeno, L.M. Reder and H.A. Simon (2000), "Perspectives on Learning, Thinking, and Activity", *Educational Researcher,* Vol. 29, pp. 11-13.

Barrows, H. (1986), "A Taxonomy of Problem Based Learning Methods", *Medical Education*, Vol. 20, pp. 481-486.

Bentley, T. and R. Miller (2004), "Personalisation; Creating the Ingredients for Systematic and Society-wide Change", a paper presented in Personalised Learning Conference, London, 17-18 May (see Chapter 8).

Bereiter, C. and M. Scardamalia (1989), "Intentional Learning as a Goal of Instruction", in L.B. Resnick (eds.), *Knowing, Learning, and Instruction. Essays in Honour of Robert Glaser*, Lawrence Erlbaum Associates, Hillsdale, NJ, pp. 361-392.

Blumenfeld, P., E. Soloway, R. Marx, J. Krajcik, M. Guzdial and A. Palincsar (1991), "Motivating Project-based Learning", *Educational Psychologist*, Vol. 26, pp. 369-398.

Boekarts, M., P.R. Pintrich and M. Zeidner (eds.) (2000), *Handbook of Self-Regulation*, Academic Press, San Diego, CA.

Brandsford, J., A.L. Brown and R.R. Cocking (eds) (2000), *How People Learn: Brain, Mind, Experience, and School*, National Academy Press, Washington D.C.

Brandsford, J.D. and B.S. Stein (1993), *The Ideal Problem Solver* (2nd ed.), Freeman, New York.

Brophy, J. (1999), "Toward a Model of the Value Aspects of Motivation in Education: Developing Appreciation for Particular Learning Domains and Activities", *Educational Psychologist*, Vol. 34, pp. 75-85.

Brown, A.L. (1997), "Transforming Schools into Communities of Thinking and Learning about Serious Matters", *American Psychologist*, Vol. 52, pp. 399-413.

Cognition and Technology Group at Vanderbilt (1992), "The Jasper Series as an Example of Anchored Instruction: Theory, Program Description, and Assessment Data", *Educational Psychologist*, Vol. 27, pp. 231-315.

Dillenbourg, P. (1999), "Introduction: What do you Mean by Collaborative Learning?", in P. Dillenbourg (eds.), *Collaborative Learning: Cognitive and Computational Approaches*, Pergamon, Amsterdam, pp. 1-19.

Guzdial, M. (1998), "Technological Support for Project-based Learning", in C. Dede (eds.), *ASCD Yearbook: Learning with Technology*, Association for supervision and curriculum development, Alexandria, VA, pp. 47-71.

Hakkarainen, K., L. Lipponen and S. Järvelä (2002), "Epistemology of Inquiry and Computer-supported Collaborative Learning", in T. Koschmann, N. Miyake and R. Hall (eds.), *CSCL2: Carrying Forward the Conversation*, Erlbaum, Mahwah, NJ, pp. 129-156.

Hakkarainen, K. and M. Sintonen (2002), "Interrogative Model of Inquiry and Computer-Supported Collaborative Learning", *Science & Education*, Vol. 11(1), pp. 25-43.

Hickey, D.T., A.L. Moore and J.W. Pellegrino (2001), "The Motivational and Academic Consequences of Elementary Mathematics Environments: Do Constructivist Innovations and Reforms Make a Difference?", *American Educational Research Journal*, Vol. 38, pp. 611-652.

Khaili, A. and L. Shashaani (1994), "The Effectiveness of Computer Applications: A Meta-analysis", *Journal of Research on Computing in Education*, Vol. 27, pp. 48–61.

Koschmann, T., A.C. Kelson, P.J. Feltovich and H.S. Barrows (1996), "Computer-supported Problem-based Learning: A Principled Approach to the Use of Computer in Collaborative Learning", in T. Koschmann (ed.), *CSCL: Theory and Practice of an Emerging Paradigm*, Lawrence Erlbaum Associates, Mahwah, NJ, pp. 1-23.

Krajcik, J., P.C. Blumenfeld, R.W. Marx, K.M. Bass, J. Fredricks and E. Soloway (1998), "Inquiry in Project-based Science Classrooms: Initial Attempts by Middle School Students", *The Journal of the Learning Sciences*, Vol. 7(3&4), pp. 313-350.

Lehtinen, E, M. Sinko and K. Hakkarainen (2001), "ICT in Finnish Education: How to Scale up Best Practices?", *International Journal of Educational Policy*, Vol. 2 (1), pp. 214-232.

Ministry of Education (2000), "Information Strategy for Education and Research 2000-2004, Implementation Plan", Ministry of Education, Helsinki.

Niemivirta, M. and S. Järvelä (2003), "Tools for Life-Long Learning: The Growing Emphasis on Learning-to-Learn Competencies and ICT in Adolescence Education in Finland", in F. Pajares and T. Urdan (eds.), *Volume III of Adolescence and Education: An International Perspective*.

Roschelle, J. and R. Pea (2002), "A Walk on the WILD Side: How Wireless Hand-helds May Change CSCL", in G. Stahl (ed.), *Proceedings of the CSCL (Computer Supported Collaborative Learning) 2002*, Erlbaum, Hillsdale, NJ.

Savery, J. and T. Duffy (1996), "Problem Based Learning: An Instructional Model and its Constructivist Framework", in B. Wilson (ed.), *Constructivist Learning Environments: Case Studies in Instructional Design*, Educational Technology Publications, Englewood Cliffs, NJ, pp. 135-148.

Scardamalia, M. and C. Bereiter (1994), "Computer Support for Knowledge Building Communities", *The Journal of the Learning Sciences*, Vol. 1, pp. 37-68.

Sinko, M. and E. Lehtinen (1999), *The Challenge of ICT in Finnish Education*, Atena, Jyväskylä.

Sternberg, R.J. (2003), "What is an 'Expert Student?'", *Educational Researcher*, Vol. 32, 8, pp. 5-9.

Sternberg, R.J. and E.L. Grigorenko (2000), *Teaching for Successful Intelligence*, Skylight Training and Publishing, Arlington Heights, IL.

Strijbos, J-W, P.A. Kirschner and R.L. Martens (eds.) (2004), *What We Know about CSCL in Higher Education*, Kluwer, Boston, MA.

Veermans, M. and S. Järvelä (2004), "Generalized Learning Goals and Situational Coping in Inquiry Learning", *Instructional Science*, Vol. 32, 4, pp. 269-291.

Volet, S. and S. Järvelä (2001) (eds.), *Motivation in Learning Contexts: Theoretical Advances and Methodological Implications*, Pergamon/Elsevier, London.

Wasson, B., S. Ludvigsen and U. Hoppe (eds.) (2003), *Designing for Change in Networked Learning Environments*, Kluwer Academic Publishers, Dordrecht.

Chapter 3
Brain Research and Learning over the Life Cycle

by
Manfred Spitzer[*]

Spitzer's argument is that brain research not only shows that we are born for learning and do it for our entire life, but also shows the conditions for successful learning and differences in learning at different stages of life. The time has come, he says, to use this understanding for shaping the learning environments and learning programmes; we can no longer afford to treat the most important resource that we have, our brain, as if we knew nothing about how it works. Thus, it is important to create the conditions for transferring insights from basic studies of learning in brain research to the practice of teaching. His discussion is organised around the following themes: from examples to rules; mechanisms for learning; phases, stages and windows; schooling and learning for life; emotions and learning; the decreasing rate of learning with age; learning, age and wisdom.

Since the times of reflex physiology, in the first decades of the last century, learning has been the quintessential subject of brain research. This chapter will show that brain research is a necessary foundation for understanding learning processes, including ways that schooling could be more effectively personalised. We are able to learn for our entire lifetime, and indeed are required to do so, so I will draw on examples from the entire human lifespan.

Some readers might consider the connection between the two main terms of the title, namely brain research and learning, a bridge too far. They might argue that brain research is still in its infancy, is about abstract domains, such as single cells, synapses, transmitters, receptors and ion currents and thus much too removed from the classroom. This is not the case

---

[*] Medical Director, Professor and Chairman of the Psychiatric Hospital at the University of Ulm, Germany.

and there is an urgent need to include the findings of brain research in profound reflections about shaping *learning environments* – a term I use for everything that has to do with learning – from different school types and curricula, to classrooms, to the relationship between learner and teacher.

The brain is always learning

Most people associate learning with school, with memorising and cramming, with sweat and frustration, bad grades and exhausting examinations; let's face it, learning has a negative image. It is considered unpleasant and people feel the need to reward themselves for learning ("one piece of chocolate for every word of French vocabulary"). It is a pity that learning theory, deriving from psychology in the middle of the last century, also comes with this view, and this has an important consequence. For, on this view there is no learning during leisure time; learning is work and as such is separated from leisure activities. Furthermore, in our culture as students we separate the day into time which we unfortunately have to spend in school (university, professional school, further education, etc.), and leisure time during which we are free and do not have to learn anything.

This view, however, does not correspond to the nature of learning. As the wings of the albatross and the fins of the whale are optimally adapted to the characteristics of air and water, like density or viscosity, our brain is optimally adapted to learning. Therefore, our brain does not learn somehow and incidentally, more or less well, or only when it has to do so. From an evolutionary perspective, the human brain has evolved to do nothing else better than learning and to prefer nothing else to it! In fact, the brain is always learning, whenever it processes information. The sceptical teacher may interrupt: "the brain is always learning and has fun with it. What an outlandish theory! I see 25 counterexamples every morning when I enter my classroom!" That someone might say this only proves my case, *i.e.*, how much we have neglected, and still neglect, the scientific insights of brain research in the realm of schools.

From examples to rules

Humans are born to learn: all babies are a living proof of that. They are the best at learning, are made for learning, and cannot be stopped. Two-year-olds do not behave like reflex robots or containers to be filled with facts. Instead, they actively try to understand their environment by examining it with little tests – quite similar to scientists – and proofing hypotheses about how things really are. Three-year-olds learn a new word every 90 minutes, and at the age of five, children know not only thousands of words in their mother tongue, but also the use of their language and its complicated grammar.

At kindergarten-age, German children know for example that verbs with the ending "–ieren" form the past tense without the prefix "ge-". Thus when they use the past tense of the verb "spazieren", (to "stroll" in English), they say: "wir sind spaziert" ("we strolled") instead of "wir sind ge-spaziert". In contrast, when they want to say that they walked ("to walk"= "laufen" in German), they say "wir sind gelaufen", knowing that they have to build the past tense of the verb "laufen" with the prefix "ge-". One could argue that the children had picked up the participles as well as the infinitive forms of the verbs, and thus learned them by heart. But this is not the case, as a simple experiment can show. We tell the children a story using some verbs that do not exist in German, and afterwards ask them about the story and find out how they build the past tense of these verbs. For example, we could tell a story about dwarfs who "quangen" and "patieren". If we ask them what the dwarfs did, they say that the dwarf "sind gequangt" and "sind patiert" (without "ge-"). That children are able to juggle grammatically with words which do not exist is proof that they learned a rule, and didn't merely memorise thousands of examples. But no one taught this rule to the children: *they generated it by themselves.* Brains have the ability to generate rules from examples. All that is needed, therefore, are the right examples – lots and lots of them.

To use an English example, when children learn the past tense, they start with frequent words they hear a lot, and thereby learn single examples: be/was/were, have/had, go/went, etc. After a while, the language production parts of their brain have done more than rote memorisation, so the children will use the ending -ed to form the past tense of words, even if they have never heard the words before. But they may also say something like "haved" or even "wented", even though they have never heard this before. So they have, without any explicit knowledge about it, found out about the rule and used it.

After language acquisition, learning really gets off the ground: school, apprenticeship, university, lifelong further education, maybe from time to time a new activity field, a foreign language, a new hobby, or simply a new environment, spatially or socially. We are constantly learning, throughout our entire life. Consequently, brain research shows that the principle – "the brain by itself constructs rules based on examples" – is valid for the entire lifespan, even if it must be supplemented by further rules.

Our brain is always learning. It weighs about 1.4 kg, which is only about 2% of the body weight. However, it uses more than 20% of the energy that we supply with food. Thereby, it not only processes information day and night, but also chooses which information is worth storing, in order to be better prepared for reaction and action in the outside world in the future. Nerve cells differ from other types of cells of the skin, muscle, or glands in that they *represent* something. I do not mean "representation" metaphorically but instead literally as an account of what a neuron is doing. A neuron is active exactly when a certain input is present, like touching a body part, hearing a word, or recognising a location. Information is processed within the nervous system in the form of action potentials, which have no qualities other than being present or absent. These signals do not smell and they have no colour; they are not even small or big. Neurons receive signals either from the sensory organs – analog-digital transducers that produce output signals from the input of physical characteristics of the environment – or from other neurons.

At synapses incoming electrical signals are chemically transferred to the receiving neuron. The point of synapses is that they are of different strength, *i.e.*, neurons receive signals via stronger or weaker connections. Depending on the strength of the transmission, the same input signal can activate one neuron but not another.

The human brain contains in the order of 100 billion (10^{11}) neurons and each neuron has up to 10 thousand connections, of which less than ten are to the same neuron, such that each neuron is connected with a thousand other neurons. So there are, approximately, 100 trillion connections (10^{14}). As neurons work by representing something, and as this means that there must be 10^{14} finely-tuned synapses in our brains, the question arises of how this is achieved. The answer is simple: Everybody does it by him- or herself! From a neurobiological point of view, all learning occurs via changes in the strength of such neuronal connections at synapses. As synapses change when they transmit signals, learning occurs whenever the brain processes information. Thus, learning is not a process that the brain needs to manage *in addition to* perception, thinking and feeling, but instead occurs automatically whenever the brain is perceiving, thinking or feeling.

Mechanisms for learning individual items and general patterns

We are able to learn single facts as well as the general rules and connections: we learn words as well as grammar, individual places as well as geometry. We learn to know individual people and general psychology. When we learn single items (people, places, words, events), the hippocampus is the part of the brain which is the most important for this type of learning, in contrast with the cortex which is engaged in extracting rules. The hippocampus is a small structure that lies deep in the temporal lobe.

Neurons in the hippocampus can be directly observed when learning new contents. When a rodent learns to find its way around an unfamiliar environment, new representations of that environment are created in the hippocampus. In humans, learning vocabulary – similar to learning new environments in rodents – depends on the creation of representations in the hippocampus. The hippocampus learns important and new details quickly. 11 September 2001 will stay in the memory of most of us quite well, when two airplanes hijacked by terrorists crashed into the two towers of the World Trade Center in New York City. Where were you when you first heard about it? Who was with you? With whom did you talk about it for the first time? Most people are able to answer these questions easily, but can't remember the afternoon of the most recent September 11 – even though it happened much closer to the present. The hippocampus stores details only when they fulfil two qualities: novelty and significance. We only have to hear important news once to remember it.

In contrast with the hippocampus, the cortex is more like a "rule-extraction-machine". The synaptic connections between its neurons only change a tiny bit during a learning episode. That is why we are unable to remember most of our impressions later on. The fact that our brain does not record events as a video-recorder would, but rather extracts the rules underlying the events, is advantageous for several reasons. First, less storage capacity is needed if just the rules are stored and not every single event. Secondly, past coincidences are not useful for the guidance of future behaviour but past rules are. By definition, coincidences will be different tomorrow from what they have been today so they are of no help in the future. And so the brain would waste resources if it stored them.

Take an example: you probably have already eaten or seen thousands of tomatoes during your lifetime, but you are unable to remember every single tomato. Why should you? Then your brain would be full of tomatoes! And these would be totally useless, when you come across the next tomato. Only your *general* knowledge about tomatoes is useful in order to deal adequately with this tomato. Tomatoes are edible, they taste good, they can be processed into ketchup, and so forth – you know all of this because you have already come across a lot of tomatoes, of which you remember only the general and structural characteristics.

Therefore, in many cases the learning of single facts or events is not only unnecessary, but also unfavourable. With the exception of places, people, and important events of personal life, the knowledge of details is otherwise not very helpful. Fortunately, we do not learn every single detail. On the contrary, our brain – except for the hippocampus, which is specialised in details – is interested in learning general rules and categories, and this not by *memorising* them but by the processing of examples and extracting generalities. This is what the brain is doing anyway because this is what we need to do to survive. When something learned in school can be applied later in life, it is mostly of this general structure – it is a rule, a general connection, acquired and strengthened by usage through many examples. Just because it is general, it not only concerns the examples, but can also be applied to new matters. This is in strong contrast to learning single facts, such as the highest mountain of Greenland, the Gross National Product of Nigeria, the birth date of Mozart, or the citric acid cycle. Such facts are useless for the everyday problems of life.

This idea is stressed in recent discussions when it is proposed we should teach "competencies", "cultural techniques" and "problem-solving strategies" instead of facts. But it is important to keep in mind that the general is learned by examples, and not through the learning of rules. Hence, practising with many examples should be an important part of every school day. Or, expressed the other way round, if facts cannot be used as examples for a more general context, it is better to do without them.

Phases, stages, and windows

Some things can be learned at different times during the lifetime of the learning organism. In ducks, imprinting happens after birth; in songbirds, singing is learned around puberty; and in nut-storing birds, the storage techniques are learned during childhood. As human beings have a long developmental period until they reach adulthood, we may infer that there are quite a number of phases, or stages of learning, or critical periods, or windows of opportunity.

And this is in fact what we do find in real people. There are different learning phases during the lifespan of a person, and they exist for different reasons. First, the brain of the newborn is still quite immature, *i.e.* it develops while it learns. This means, secondly, that early learning is especially meaningful. Third, the rate of learning decreases with increasing age. And fourth, the one who already knows something learns differently from the one who starts from the beginning. The brain of a newborn contains practically all neurons, but many of them are not yet or only slightly linked. As all learning consists of a change in the connections between neurons, this has important consequences, which are being looked at only recently in the field of cognitive developmental neurobiology. Let us look at some examples.

The environment of a newborn is very complex. When it learns something, it would make sense if it learned simple matters first and more and more complex ones afterwards. Learning complexity is based upon already-learned simplicity. How can the baby learn anything under these circumstances? The answer from cognitive neuroscience is astonishing: the newborn learns so well precisely because its brain is still immature. At first, its brain works in the simplest manner and hence is only able to process the simplest rules. And thus, it is only able to learn these. Once they are learned, other mechanisms take care that what has been learned will not then be forgotten. At the same time the brain develops, *i.e.* new connections are created which allow the processing of more complex contexts. Those are added to the very simple things and so on. Thus, the newborn does not need a teacher who prepares learning materials didactically, because its brain is still developing. Consider language development – if we had had our adult brain already at birth, we would have been unable to learn something as complex as language. And, the time window of language acquisition appears to close at around age 12 or 13, so that if someone has not learned how to talk by then, they never will.

We know that the representations – the neurons that code for something particular – are not just distributed randomly in the brain. The cortex by itself has the ability to create *maps* of representations. We speak of a "map" because neurons, which represent something similar, are located closely together and that events that occur often are represented by more neurons than events that occur rarely. The development of these "maps" depends on experience so that what is experienced will be represented. The best-known map is the sensory cortex, the part of the cortex which is important for the processing of touch signals coming from the body surface. As we process more touch information with our hands, lips and tongue, these body parts are represented by more neurons in the somato-sensory cortex than body parts with which we rarely process important touch information, like the back. The map, in a way, contains the statistics of the information of touch coming in. We now know that there are many maps in the cortex that are not only relevant for touch information, but also for seeing and hearing and probably also for higher cognitive functions like language, thinking, and wanting.

Furthermore, new research has demonstrated that the experience-based development of the maps is the signal for their consolidation (Chang and Merzenich, 2003). In other words, as long as no map is created, the corresponding part of the brain stays flexible. But once a map has been created based on the processing of the corresponding experiences then the consolidation cannot be, or only slightly, changed again. This explains the special importance of early experiences. It also determines how much capacity for processing (*i.e.* cortical hardware) is created for certain representations. If someone did not use her or his hands for the first three years of life, he or she would be able to use them to touch later, but the touch would not be as precise as it could have been. On the other hand, if someone learns to play guitar as a child, touching often very precisely with the fingers of the left hand, (s)he will have a few centimetres more for the representation of his(her) left hand in his(her) adult brain (Elbert *et al.* 1995).

The developing brain is the cause for the existence of learning phases, stages, periods, or windows. We still know relatively little but we do have a field – developmental cognitive neuroscience – devoted to it. Its results should be of great importance for shaping the learning environment.

Schooling and learning for life

We do not learn for the school, but for life. This educational principle is more important today than ever. In schools 150 years ago, students already learned for their lives. But at that time, it was known more or less what life looked like and which knowledge was to be used. One hundred years ago, there was considerable certainty about what students should learn – their mother tongue, mathematics, physics, chemistry, languages, etc. Now we know that the world looked very different only 30 years later. Not only were there cars, planes, radios and telegraphs, but also eugenics, new kinds of poverty, unemployment, social problems, recession and new global policies. A person in 1900, who thought that he/she knew what students should learn to be fit for life, was mistaken.

Nowadays we are smarter in one respect – we know that we do not know what life will be like in 30 years time. By implication we do not know if something which is learned in school today will be useful then. And progress appears, if anything, to happen at an ever faster pace. Hence, the above-mentioned principle has become *more important and at the same time more uncertain* than ever. How can we make sure that material is really learned for life? With this in mind, people often reason as follows: because of rapid change and the accompanying uncertainties, the learning of facts in school is becoming obsolete. Rather, problem-solving strategies are important – the knowledge of general rules and skills, not details and facts, which can be applied to different problems, even those unknown today. These skills should be so general and basic, that people speak of the acquisition of "meta-cognitive basic competencies" and the like.

This sounds plausible but on closer scrutiny it turns out to be too general and shallow. Neuro-scientific studies of the mechanisms of learning in human beings allow for more precise analysis of how to connect schooling and learning. For instance, we now have insights on how to improve the prospects that what is learned in school will result in long-lasting skills that can be applied to practice-orientated problem solving throughout life.

Emotions and learning

A recent study (Erk *et al.*, 2003) of the role of emotions in learning has shown for the first time that *neutral* material is stored in different parts of the brain, depending on the emotional state of the learner when the material was learned. This study examined brain activity with functional magnetic resonance imaging (fMRI) during the encoding of words. We wanted to find out if memory performance for neutral words differed for learning in a positive, neutral or negative emotional state, and if different brain regions are involved for each case. In order to do so, we set up an experiment, consisting of many trials that were carried out in the scanner. In each trial, subjects were first presented with a picture, which conjured up positive, negative or neutral emotions. Then a neutral word was presented, and the subject's task was to indicate, by pressing one of two buttons, whether the word denoted something abstract or concrete. This decision process ensured that subjects actually paid attention to the words and processed their meaning. This series of presentation was repeated many times while subjects lay in the magnetic resonance tomograph. Afterwards they were asked to freely recall the words, and to write them down.

The results were stunning. First, we could demonstrate that the emotional context in which word storage happened does influence subsequent memory performance. Words that were stored in a positive emotional context were remembered the best. Moreover, we were also able to show that activity in various brain regions allowed us to predict whether or not a word would be remembered, depending on the emotional context under which the words were learned. Storing words embedded in a positive emotional context caused activity in the hippocampus and the para-hippocampus, *i.e.*, in areas related to learning and memory. In contrast, when words were encoded under a negative emotional context, the amygdala was active.

What does this mean for learning in schools? The hippocampus mediates learning of events. We know that events do not reside in the hippocampus for ever, but rather get transferred to the cortex within the ensuing days (in mice), weeks (in rats) and months (in human beings). In other words, the learned material is transferred from the fast-learning hippocampus to the "slower learner," the cortex, the brain's long-term storage device. The function of the amygdala is totally different. It contributes to fast learning and the future avoidance of unpleasant events. If the amygdala is destroyed in a rat on both sides of the brain, the rat can still learn to orientate in a maze using the hippocampus, but does not learn fear. In order to learn fear, humans as well as rats need the amygdala.

When the amygdala is activated, heart rate and blood pressure rise and the muscles contract: we are afraid and are prepared for fight or flight – a useful response in regard to imminent danger. However, the effects not only concern the body, but also the mind. When the lion comes from the left, we run to the right. The individual, who leans back and starts thinking laterally and creatively, does not live long. Fear produces a certain cognitive style that facilitates the execution of simple learned routines but at the same time, it blocks creativity. This made sense 100 000 years ago, but nowadays it often leads to problems. For someone with anxiety during an exam, it may be impossible to find a creative solution that would be easily identified when not in an anxious emotional state. Someone who is anxious will easily find him or herself "stuck" in a situation and incapable of "freeing the mind". When there is no anxiety, thoughts become more open, associations run freely, and new solutions to old problems pop into our minds. This fits with the subjective experience of most people and has also been demonstrated scientifically.

As the amygdala has the function to prepare us for fight and flight, its activation leads to mental changes that do not foster creative problem-solving. This means that if we want our children to learn for life in school, we need to make sure that the emotional atmosphere is right during learning. Our results not only show that learning works best in a pleasant atmosphere, but also why learning should only occur in a pleasant atmosphere. Personalisation, as is discussed elsewhere in this volume, may be one avenue for creating such positive learning contexts, particularly in light of the changes taking place in what people need to learn.

The decreasing rate of learning with age

"What little Hans has not learned, big Hans will never learn" is a German saying. And from many studies we know that indeed with increasing age, there is a decrease in the speed of learning processes and of its neuronal correlate, neuro-plasticity. Upon closer consideration, the decreasing learning rate with increasing age makes a lot of sense. All learning is a result of the change in the strength of synaptic transmission. In neural network models of learning, the amount of change in synaptic strength per single experience is expressed by a number, a so-called *learning constant*. A small learning constant, implementing learning in small steps, assures that things are not forgotten. Moreover, it avoids learning too quickly and thereby over-shooting the goal (*i.e.*, the true value of whatever has to be learned). So, in order to learn something precisely, learning has to be slow. Finally, learning in small steps makes sure that every single experience contributes only to a small extent to whatever is learned, such that the *general structures* of these experiences are learned through many repetitions, rather than single coincidental (and useless) features.

Such slow learning, however, contradicts the general demand for fast learning as dictated by evolution. The reason why learning should occur quickly is clear for every organism, so far as accessing nutritional resources or life-saving reactions in dangerous situations are concerned. Thus, organisms should learn slowly, in order to not forget and to generalise and to be precise, and quickly in order not to starve or be eaten up while still learning.

This contradiction is solved in living systems (as well as in artificial neural networks and in robotics) through initial fast learning followed by ever slower learning. Hence, the rate of learning must decline with increasing age for learning to occur optimally. The reason why children are fast learners and older people are slow learners is quite simple. For organisms to survive better in their environment, they need to get to know it better, so it is good to learn quickly first and then more slowly. This enables organisms to better estimate the true parameters of the environment in a short time, and then later get closer and closer to the true parameters. Transferred to humans, this implies that elderly people know many things much better than youngsters. It is not a coincidence that we speak of "old masters" with respect to people who have acquired knowledge over a lifetime.

The idea of a declining learning rate with age presupposes that learning occurs in a stable environment. However, given that our environment changes so quickly, the prerequisite of a stable environment is not any more given in many fields. Thus it is possible that people find themselves in a situation where the values, which they filtered out from their environment, are not valid any more, or that they learned skills, which are of no more use. The old master of building violins will be very good at that task but has great difficulty learning how to build synthesizers.

There are, however, fields, which basically do not change – mothers love their children, husbands their wives, grandparents their grandchildren, etc. – and some aspects of our social life are culturally quite stable through time and space. In contrast, science and technology are full of sweeping changes. Therefore, we should expect that it is at different points of the human life-span when someone is able to make contributions to these fields. And indeed, fundamental discoveries in mathematics and physics are made by young people: a 20-year-old mathematician, for example, invented group theory in a single night; physics in the 1920s was also known as the physics of the "twenties" (Heidenberg, Pauli, Schrödinger and the like), because at that time, young people caused our world-view to totter and changed our understanding of things. Fast learning, novelty-seeking, a fast Central Processing Unit, and lots of empty RAM, but no necessity of having loads of data stored on the hard drive (to use computing metaphors), is what it takes to be excel in maths and physics.

Learning, age and wisdom

It is quite different in the social sciences where great achievements are not made by 20-year-olds but by those in their 50s and 60s. It is not difficult to guess why this is the case for we are always learning in the field of social interaction. People – in contrast to the technical things that surround us – do not change so quickly. Accordingly, we learn to understand them better and better and become wiser in dealing with them. Theories in the social sciences and reflections on ethics and political issues are therefore rather the domain of older people. This does not mean that young people cannot, or should not, think about these things. But older people are in a better position than younger ones to assess socio-political problems. It makes sense that most constitutions provide people with the right to vote for president before they have the right to become president; people who are awarded the Nobel Peace Prize are much older at the time of their achievements than physicists at the time of theirs.

Older people learn more slowly than youngsters, but in contrast they have already learned a great deal and are able to use their acquired knowledge for the integration of new knowledge. The more one knows, the better one is able to link new concepts with already established knowledge. Since learning consists of the creation of such links, older people indeed have an advantage. Knowledge can help to structure new knowledge, to order and anchor it.

But knowledge can also make us blind to the things that are in front of our eyes. For older people, it is therefore important to stay open minded and to use the knowledge that they have already acquired for future learning. Older people do not learn facts as easily as younger people; they need anchoring points. And those points must fit their experiences. This is not easy to realise, as the practice in many companies shows when they try to teach new things to their employees the same way for everybody. No wonder this works the best with young employees and the worst with older ones. This is often used as an argument in favour of youth, but by not starting the teaching for older employees with what they already know, a lot of useful knowledge is not exploited. This knowledge can be important whenever a new problem has to be solved creatively. So, the question of who is better at learning, the younger or the older person, cannot be generally answered.

That learning at an older age is not a recent phenomenon linked to the inverted population pyramid may be illustrated by the following two examples. Walker and co-workers investigated the Arche tribe in Eastern Paraguay. The male Arche leave their settlements for a few days in order to hunt with other members of the tribe in the woods. They only use their hands, machetes, bows and arrows, with no guns or other modern weapons. At the age of 24 years, the people of this tribe reach their best physical fitness. How old are the ones who bring back home most of the meat? Since the beginning of the 1980s, researchers took notes on which member of the tribe killed what prey. As a result, a clear dependence of the success in hunting and age was found – the men who brought home the most prey were about 40 years old. Competitions in archery showed the same age dependency as the success in hunting. The number of hits increased until the age of about 40 and then stayed constant for the subsequent two decades. The same result was found for recognition of tracks. But in trying to teach archery – in a six-week crash course – to the members of the tribe that did not go hunting any more, they had not the slightest success.

It became clear that with hunting as with playing soccer, violin, or chess, performance is best after practising for at least two decades. If lifelong learning is so important for people who live under Stone Age-like circumstances, what about in today's society based upon knowledge and information? We tend to lay off the 50-year-old and employ the 24-year-old. This would have been a mistake even in the Stone Age! In today's society, which is based on knowledge and skills, this can only be extremely short-sighted.

A second example is about grandmothers not grandfathers. London-based anthropologists (Sear, Mace and McGregor, 2000) found in a study carried out in Gambia that the presence of the grandmother in a family led to the doubling of infant survival to adulthood, and another study demonstrated grandmother-dependent increases in fertility (Sear, Mace and McGregor, 2003). Data from Finland and Canada and on the survival of human beings over generations, taken from old records in the 18th and 19th century, lead to the same conclusion (Lahdenperä et al., 2004). Even studies in elephants and apes point in the same direction. In elephants, the age of the matriarch (the oldest female in a group of ten to a dozen females) is highly correlated with the fertility of the younger members of the group (McComb et al., 2001), while the grandmother making sure that the mother takes care of her new baby has been observed in gorillas (Nakamichi et al., 2004). These studies clarify the value of old age for species that live in groups. When there are no written records, let alone the Internet, then older individuals are the only source of information and experience which is healthy for the reproductive success of the entire group.

Summing up and based on characteristics in information-processing at different stages of life, it is an advantage when people of different ages live and work together. The older person has a larger and more profound basis of knowledge, the younger person has a better working memory and faster processing speed. If a problem is intensely studied by such a community, the probability of a solution is maximal. Observations from the field of anthropology show that even simple cultures appreciate life experience. The challenge for our society is the transfer of these facts into our everyday life. If aging is seen as an annoying problem of a population pyramid that stands on its head, this possibility has already been lost. Older people should not only be conscious of their value but also of their function. They surely will not fulfil their value and function just by playing golf or cards!

Conclusion

Brain research not only shows that we are born for learning and do it for our entire life. It also shows the conditions for successful learning and differences in learning at different stages of life. The time has come for us to use this understanding for shaping the learning environments and learning programmes. We can no longer afford to treat the most important resource that we have, our brain, as if we knew nothing about how it works. Brain research is still in its early stages and we know relatively little, but the little we know is important for improving learning processes.

Medicine offers one model of how the application of basic science to practical use can be made a reality. Today's discussion about the funding of medical treatment is possibly the best indicator for its success: everyone wants medical treatment of the highest level. Medicine reached this point as it moved from anecdotes (expert X says this will help the best) to evidence (study Y shows which treatment is best). Evidence-based medicine is not about what someone says, but what we know for sure. A drug or procedure A is better than a drug or procedure B, because investigations have shown it.

In medicine, the mechanism of action of a drug is distinguished from its clinical effect. Similarly, a science of education that has been informed by brain sciences should distinguish between mechanisms of learning, on the one hand, and effectiveness of the learning environment, on the other. It is one thing to know which biochemical pathways a drug acts upon, and another to know how many patients with the illness X are better off with that drug as opposed to a placebo.

The science of education should progress in the same way: it is not only important to investigate the basics of learning processes with brain research, but also to examine the possibilities of application, efficacy, and possible side effects. Medicine as a science and an art lives from basic science and practical application through which it becomes clear what helps and what does not, which theories are useful and which not, which processes are important and which not. Theory alone does not show this.

Thus, it is important to create the conditions for transferring insights from basic studies of learning in brain research to the practice of teaching. In addition to basic research, applied research is necessary and should preferably be conducted by those who do basic research as well (like in medicine), or at least in cooperation with them. This is where I see an important connection to the explorations of personalisation in the public sector and more specifically in education. Personalisation implies, at least in part, a strong integration of theory and practice – or learning through doing. Even though we still know relatively little about brain functioning, we know enough to bet on the fruitfulness of personalised learning with one way of getting started to be through a neuroscience-based understanding of education.

References

Barinaga, M. (2000), "A Critical Issue for the Brain", *Science 288*, pp. 2116-2119.

Chang, E.F. and M.M. Merzenich (2003), "Environmental Noise Retards Auditory Cortical Development", *Science 300*, pp. 498-502.

Elbert, T., C. Pantev, C. Wienbruch, B. Rockstroh and E. Taub (1995), "Increased Use of the Left Hand in String Players Associated with Increased Cortical Representation of the Fingers", *Science 220*, pp. 21-23.

Erk, S., M. Kiefer, J. Grothe, A.P. Wunderlich, M. Spitzer and H. Walter (2003), "Emotional Context Modulates Subsequent Memory Effect", *NeuroImage 18*, pp. 439-447.

Kinsley, C.H. *et al.* (1999), "Motherhood Improves Learning and Memory", *Nature 402*, pp. 137-138.

Lahdenperä, M, V. Lummaa, S. Helle, M. Tremblay and A.F. Russell (2004), "Fitness Benefits of Prolonged Post-reproductive Lifespan in Women", *Nature 428*, pp. 178-181.

Lundborg, G. and B. Rosén (2001), "Tactile Gnosis after Nerve Repair", *The Lancet 258*, p. 809.

McComb, K. *et al.* (2001), "Matriarchs as Repositories of Social Knowledge in African Elephants", *Science 292*, pp. 491-494.

Nakamichi, M., A. Silldorff, C. Bringham and B. Sexton (2004), "Baby-transfer and other Interactions between its Mother and Grandmother in a Captive Social Group of Lowland Gorillas", *Primates 45*, pp. 73-77.

Sear, R., R. Mace and I.A. McGregor (2000), "Maternal Grandmothers Improve the Nutritional Status and Survival of Children in Rural Gambia. Proceedings of the Royal Society of London. Series B", *Biological Sciences 267*, pp. 461-467.

Sear, R., R. Mace and I.A. McGregor (2003), "The Effects of Kin on Female Fertility in Rural Gambia", *Evolution and Human Behavior 24*, pp. 25-42.

Spitzer, M. (2000), "Geist im Netz", Spektrum Akademischer Verlag, Heidelberg.

Spitzer, M. (2002a), "Lernen", Spektrum Akademischer Verlag, Heidelberg.

Spitzer, M. (2002b), "Musik im Kopf", Schattauer, Stuttgart.

Spitzer, M. (2003), "Verdacht auf Psyche", Schattauer, Stuttgart.

Walker, R. *et al.* (2002), "Age-dependency in Hunting Ability among the Ache of Eastern Paraguay", *Journal of Human Evolution 42*, pp. 639-657.

Chapter 4
Personalised Learning and
Changing Conceptions of Childhood and Youth

by
Yvonne Hébert and William J. Hartley[*]

Hébert and Hartley take the example of Canada as indicative of changing conceptions of youth that occur through societies, shaped by moral, socio-economic, political and legal influences. These include the appearance of a more liberal Christianity, the growth of industrial and agricultural productivity, the spread of literacy and the rise of the middle class, the greater emancipation of women, and enlarged notions of citizenship. Two particular processes – the advent of mass schooling and the post-war development of teenage youth culture in advertising and through the media – have been instrumental in extending childhood and shaping youth. Educational policy makers and researchers have a responsibility to understand conceptions of children and youth and to recognise the forces that shape them and young people must be recognised as whole. Educators are called upon to see beyond broad social representations of children and youth so as to support their strengths, legitimacy, diversity and vitality.

There are many childhoods. What is meant by conceptions of "child" and "youth" has changed over time and in different historical contexts. In each major period in history, there have been different ideas about what children are like and how best to teach and socialise them. Today, these images are shifting in new directions – towards new definitions that challenge our fundamental conceptions not only of childhood and youth but also of the state. As we progress towards the knowledge society, the mass conception of children is shifting to a more individualistic approach. Dramatic societal shifts result in conflicting positions, policies, and

---

[*] Respectively, Professor in the Faculty of Education, University of Calgary, Canada, and educator with the Calgary Board of Education.

practices. When considering the reform of public service and education, it is essential to keep the fluidity of the conceptions of childhood and youth in mind for they are central to the current debate on the personalisation of education.

Identity as key to self-understanding

Educational concerns today can best be summed up by the key words *standards*, *curriculum reform*, *accountability* and *testing*. The logic is that if the bar is raised, then students will perform better. Standardised textbooks, curriculum and learning frameworks, and better teaching and learning will ensue. If schools are held accountable, educators will produce results. If students are tested to see what they know and are able to do, both teachers and students will be motivated to avoid the consequences that come with low scores. While this approach to raising student achievement has its merits and its proponents, educators who focus solely on factors that are external to students are likely to achieve only limited success. Children and youth cannot be standardised. Young people's sense of agency and of self heavily influences their self-worth and their educational performance, all of which is also socially conditioned. If young people are to succeed as thinkers, as learners, and as humans who make valuable contributions to society, more must be known about them than their scores on standardised measures of achievement.

Conceptions of childhood and youth – as socially and historically constructed representations of identities within particular economic, cultural and political contexts – are central to the success or failure of students at school (Chunn, 2003; Sadowski, 2003). Schools are probably the most important context shaping the identities of children and youth – as strong learners in particular intellectual disciplines, as athletes on a team, as citizens and members of society. How educators understand young people and how children and adolescence understand themselves is critical to their ability to comprehend themselves as social actors and to their capacity for acting upon society to achieve their intellectual and career goals as well as state-established goals, in reciprocal transformations of self, school and society. It is essential to know who young people are and how they have been constructed.

The construction of childhood – an historical perspective

Childhood, as we know it today, was invented during the modern industrial era. By the 17th century, the child was constructed as separate and distinct from the adult. Childhood ended around the age of seven, with a change of attire marking the passage to adulthood. This was consistent with the separation of mind and matter, with reason as the means for classification, order, and hierarchy, with the religious focus on the individual soul. A distinct group was created that needed protection from a corrupt society. The school became the perfect vehicle for the construction, protection and reformation of the child.

Since the 18th century, the conception of childhood encapsulated in the bourgeois family model has become increasingly dominant in Western countries (Chunn, 2003; Rooke and Schnell, 1982, 1983). The influential Jean Piaget (1896-1980) proposed that children individually construct their worlds from inside out, a process that is both self-directed and self-regulated. Piaget describes the child as a developing scientist, systematically examining problems in the real world, hypothesising and learning how to solve problems through discovery. He (1957) emphasised the mental over the active, thinking over doing, abstract over the concrete, adult over child, rationality over irrationality, and ultimately believed in the innocence of children. Throughout the 20th century and into the 21st, children and youth have been increasingly defined as subordinate and dependent upon adults. Subject to stringent monitoring and censure for engaging in adult pastimes, children and youth have also been protected from the corrupting adult influences. Thus, an originally constructivist middle-class "angelic" conception of childhood, linked to the rise of literacy and the middle class, was over-applied and universalised well beyond its social, class, cultural and philosophical roots. As such, the model contributed to a demonising conception of the child and youth as delinquent and deviant.

Historical examples from Canada

The emerging changes in the way that we think about children are congruent in the ways that we think about learning. We can write a story about Canada's history over the past three centuries that considers the changing conceptions of childhood in terms of the sense of agency, individuality, autonomy, power, emotional expression, voice, and social roles of young people.

Colonial childhood in Canada was constructed somewhat differently than in Europe. The political economy of extraction from the new world to enrich the old, the minimal influence of the church and state, and the mixed origins of the European settlers tempered the entrenchment of customs and community bonds (Janovicek, 2003, p. 35). In the new world, children were encouraged to be self-reliant in order to suit social and economic patterns of colonial life and developed new identities. Childhood and adolescence were considered life stages separate from adulthood (Moogk, 2003; Pollard, 2003).

Society changed dramatically when Canada was created as a confederated state (1867). It was a time of phenomenal population growth that included massive migration, which in turn produced new sources of tensions within Canadian society. Aboriginal populations were more and more marginalised, and existing English-French and Aboriginal conflicts were exacerbated (McLeod, 1979). From the 1870s to the 1930s, childhoods continued to be constructed in the context of economic and political ideologies, with powerful nationalising agendas that were blueprints for progress. The age of industrialisation was also the age of nationalism. Children and youth were conceptualised as cultural, economic and political commodities. Schools were the socialising agency and had become an agent of the state: public schools taught citizenship, as a form of Anglo-conformity and incipient capitalism.

In the context of a national transformation, the new social policies on the child of this era had focused on the rearing of children in family settings, maintaining and protecting health, transforming the means of schooling and education, and preventing children from becoming a burden on society (Sutherland, 2000; Coulter, 2003). These social policies were elaborated in the context of decades-long struggles and debates on public education, its purposes, practices and outcomes, informed by many school-based initiatives, progressive ideas as well as the work of professional and educational associations (Houston and Prentice, 1988). Over time, agreement developed on what was termed the "new education" in 1915 in Ontario: a) the importance of the home in shaping the next generation; b) the need for an aggressive policy of Canadianisation as part of the programme of forming and reforming society through education; c) various elements of the "new education" of the times, such as agriculture as a school subject, school gardens, manual training, domestic science, consolidated schools; and d) the widespread indifference of communities, school trustees and many teachers as the most serious obstacles to educational and social reform. These debates and reforms set the stage for the progressivism movement in Canada.

During the turmoil of the Great Depression in the Thirties, the notion of progress was itself questioned. Remarkable social and educational change ensued in the name of progressivism. The social, political and educational changes completed the transition from *laissez-faire* state of the late 19th century to a welfare state. Marked by emerging farmer-labour alliances in the 1920s, and in combination with the economic crises of the 1930s, political reorganisation occurred across Canada. Social, political and educational experimentation was rampant, and one such experiment was progressive education. The post-Second World War period also saw the re-introduction of human rights. Emerging social and economic rights included the universal rights of children to education and welfare, as an avowed national aim and international idea for post war social policy (Marshall, 2003; Bruno-Jofré, 1996).

The growing hegemony of the middle-class family pattern among Canadian working classes accompanied the development of the welfare state, set against a backdrop of an emergent corporate capitalism, rapid urbanisation and the implementation of mass democracy. This fuelled moral and social reform movements aimed at inculcating the norms associated with the bourgeois family model among so-called deviant populations (Chunn, 2003). A concern for order and a more disciplined society motivated educational reformers who called for greater social efficiency. Social reconstruction was the new goal and it lasted until the mid-century.

Modern education, then, had a number of key purposes: to teach youngsters the means for social control; to disseminate knowledge; to meet the public demand for social improvement; to meet the demand for industrial efficiency via practical subjects; and to meet the need to make each individuals into a productive social unit (Sutherland, 2002), while perpetuating identifiable values and meeting pre-determined, clear, specific ends. It was during this period that children and youth began to be conceptualised as scientific inquirers and discoverers, as participants in democracy, and as bearers of rights. This reflected a radical change in socio-political and educational thinking about young people. Challenging the bourgeois conception of childhood as a time of preparation for the future, these new conceptions recognised the historical realities of childhood in Canadian contexts and the contemporary emphasis on living in the present.

Thus, the children of the Colonial and Confederate periods were precursors of lives to come decades later, in which young people are recognised as being entitled to human dignity during their childhood and youth. Young people became subjects in the here and now, social actors who are self-motivated, cooperative individuals. Nonetheless, competing conceptions placed children and youth in positions of dependency to enforce middle-class views of young people among those who were not. This perpetuated the negative view of the bourgeois child as a dependant, possibly as a ward of court; as a recipient, unequal, marginalised and passive. The youth as radical straddled more than one conception: as social actor and citizen as well as troublemaker insisting on being treated by others certain ways.

Concerns and demands for reform formed a comprehensive attack on progressive education throughout the 1950s, and continued as profound social changes emerged in the 1960s. Some religious, political and cultural groups complained that traditional social and ethical values were being undermined. Another complaint came from universities who criticised progressive education for having abandoned all standards of rigour, treating subjects superficially, and contributing to the decline of social, ethical, and political values (Neatby, 1953). Calls for the primacy of "core" school subjects emerged. Educational mandates and systems had to keep up with the seemingly insatiable demands of industry and bureaucracy in the new technocratic society (Mazurek, 1999). Both labour and professional requirements required increased levels of technical and intellectual skills as the economy changed fundamentally. The educational response, predictably, was a return to a core of essential knowledge and disciplines, and a reaffirmation of traditional values.

The rise of prosperity in Canada in the 1960s generated a powerful momentum to economic and social changes, leading once again to educational reform. Prosperity resulted in a chronic shortage of personnel especially in technical fields and the professions, including a serious teacher shortage; an explosion in the budgets and student populations in schools and post-secondary institutions; and an increase in schooling options (Mazurek, 1999). The 1960s heralded an era of incredible social and cultural innovation and experimentation. This feeling took form, in overt rebellion against tradition and authority, in the sexual revolution and drug use, in the redefinition of identity through humanistic psychology and cooperative living arrangements, and in a more direct democratic participation in the student rights movement and demonstrations.

An increased awareness and emphasis on world affairs also permeated society as well as the schools in the 1970s and 1980s as a result of changing immigration patterns (Osborne, 1996), stemming from the introduction in 1967 of a non-racist merit system. Over a million and a half people entered the country in the decade from 1968, originating mostly from Asia and the Caribbean, with a concomitant drop of immigrants from Europe. Once dismissed, the hyphenated Canadians were here to stay.

This period heralds major shifts in changing conceptions of childhood and youth, with the Canadian Charter and the UN Convention on the Rights of Children providing their legal bases. Recognising that children need a cultural education flowed from the federal multiculturalism policy of 1971, followed in the 1990s with the recognition of rights to a cultural and linguistic education to safeguard and develop identities. With student-centred educational reforms, all marginalised groups made great strides in obtaining equity rights to self-determination and to parental control of education. The ratification of the UN Convention on the Rights of Children (CRC) provides a more general basis for conceptions of childhood and youth as social actors and active citizens, although the Convention's meanings for educational policy, curriculum and pedagogy have yet to be fully tested (Howe and Covell, 2005).

Contemporary conceptions of children and youth are more sharply drawn than in previous periods. Children and youth as consumers permeate the discourses of educational and legal reforms, along three dimensions: as labourers who produce goods and services, as consumers who spend their limited resources, and as commodities whose images and music market goods and services. The conception of children and youth as consumers within a global marketplace limits citizenship and misconstrues the power of the consumer as freedom rather than understanding it as devolving from economic pursuits of international corporations. Movies contributed to the shift of values towards the culture of personality and self-indulgence of consumerism. The demonising conception remains strong and is seen in new forms of racism which target indigenous and immigrant children and youth, as well as in the highest youth incarceration rates among the industrialised countries (Schissell, 1997; in press). Canadian youth of immigrant origin create a sense of self that is strategic, solving various types of problems that are particular to the process of integration, negotiating their differences, making friends, and accumulating social capital to facilitate their insertion into school and society. Delayed adulthood is yet another characteristic of late modern life, as none of the previous markers of passage serve today to clearly delineate adulthood.

Children and youth as learners are essential to the educational marketplace. The new student is constructed as an independent, autonomous, self-directed and self-motivated learner, in the face of serious cutbacks, lean pedagogies and support services. Yet in reality, students face class and racial differences, struggle with financial and family responsibilities, and continue to experience poverty and self-doubt. Equity is taken up as an issue of parental choice rather than as claims for the inclusion and fair treatment of the disadvantaged and minorities. Parental choice takes on the meaning of equity, as a sense of fairness underlies the offer and selection of a range of educational options, thus contributing to the maintenance of the privileges of the dominant classes.

Conclusion

To sum up, the example of Canada is indicative of changing conceptions of youth that occur through societies. It serves to illustrate the power of social norms and mores in constructing childhood. Conceptions of childhood and youth are social constructs, contingent upon a wide variety of factors and circumstances, cultural traditions and rituals, and historical variations (Hollands, 2001). Many moral, socio-economic, political and legal influences have shaped these changes. These include the appearance of a more liberal Christianity, the growth of industrial and agricultural productivity, the spread of literacy and the rise of the middle class, the greater emancipation of women, and enlarged notions of citizenship (Strong-Boag, 2002). Two particular processes – the advent of schooling at all levels, and the post-war development of teenage youth culture in advertising and through the media – have been instrumental in extending childhood and shaping youth (Hollands, 2001).

There are two dominant conceptions, an angelic one and a demonising one. One represents children and youth from the perspective of the bourgeois model of family: children and youth are dependent on adults for their basic needs, protected from predatory adults and older children, treated separately from adults, and were not to labour until maturity (Rooke and Schnell, 1983; Strong-Boag, 2002; and Chunn, 2003). The other conception stems from the over-application of the bourgeois model to youthful populations for whom it does not fit and who are blamed for this mismatch individually. Yet beyond these two are the many conceptions of childhood constructed throughout Canada's story, which become clear in particular economic, cultural and political contexts, particular configurations of power relations, and within particular spatial and temporal boundaries.

The one conception that runs through all of Canada's historical periods is the notion of children and youth as *consumers*, *i.e.*, as producers, buyers and commodities. In the colonial periods, children's labour was a survival strategy of the family, the colonisers and the fur trade. During Confederation and Western expansion into the 1920s, child labour was extensive and its excesses led to child labour laws, further supporting the middle class conception of the child as dependent upon adults and free to play rather than to labour. During the era of progressivism, the child was conceptualised as a scientific inquirer, a liberated thinker and a social actor – the middle-class view of childhood anticipating the later conception of the independent learner. The following period saw the emergence of Charter identities, individual and collective rights including francophone linguistic school rights, and a conscious construction of a society respectful of self and others. The rise of prosperity after the 1950s followed by two recessions in the 1980s and 1990s, once again made explicit the economic and political agendas, underpinning educational reforms.

Educational policy makers and researchers have a responsibility to understand conceptions of children and youth and to recognise the forces that shape them. Young people must be recognised with all their self-creating potential, as whole individuals who, as members of particular socio-political and cultural groupings, are faced with their own issues and challenges (Pacom, 2001). The lives of young people today are diverse and multifaceted. By virtue of their profession, educators are called upon to see beyond broad social representations of children and youth so as to support their strengths, legitimacy, diversity and vitality. Not all students are alike and one conception of the student/learner/consumer will not fit all. Imposing one through policy and practices will simply increase inequalities.

References

Bruno-Jofré, R. (1996), "Schooling and the Struggles to Develop a Common Policy, 1919-1971", in R. Bruno-Jofré and L. Grieger (eds.), *Papers on Contemporary Issues in Education Policy and Administration in Canada: A Foundations Perspective,* University of Manitoba, Winnipeg.

Chunn, D. (2003), "Boys Will Be Men, Girls Will Be Mothers: The Legal Regulation of Childhood in Toronto and Vancouver", in N. Janovicek and J. Parr (eds.), *Histories of Canadian Children and Youth*, Oxford University Press, Toronto.

Coulter R.P (2003), "Between School and Marriage: A Case Study Approach to Young Women's Work in Early Twentieth Century Canada", in N. Janovicek and J. Parr (eds.), *Histories of Canadian Children and Youth*, Oxford University Press, Toronto, pp. 88-99.

Hollands, R. (2001), "(Re)presenting Canadian Youth: Challenge or Opportunity?", in M. Gauthier and D. Pacom (eds.), *Spotlight on Canadian Youth Research*, Les Éditions de l'IQRC/Les Presses de l'Université Laval, Sainte-Foy.

Houston, S.E. and A. Prentice (1988), "Schooling and Scholars in Nineteenth Century Ontario", University of Toronto Press, Toronto.

Howe, R.B. and K. Covell (2005), "Empowering Children: Children's Rights Education as a Pathway to Citizenship", University of Toronto Press, Toronto.

Janovicek, N. (2003), "Colonial Childhood, 1700-1880", in N. Janovicek and J. Parr (eds.), *Histories of Canadian Children and Youth*, Oxford University Press, Toronto.

Marshall, D. (2003), "Reconstruction Politics, the Canadian Welfare State, and the Ambiguity of Children's Rights", in N. Janovicek and J. Parr (eds.), *Histories of Canadian Children and Youth*, Oxford University Press, Toronto.

Mazurek, K. (1999), "Passing Fancies: Educational Change in Alberta", in T. Harrison and J. Kachur (eds.), *Contested Classrooms: Education, Globalization and Democracy in Alberta*, Parkland Institute and University of Alberta Press, Edmonton.

McLeod, K. (1979), "Politics, Schools and the French Language, 1881-1931", in D. Jones, N. Sheehan and R. Stamp (eds.), *Shaping the Schools of the Canadian West*, Detselig, Calgary.

Moogk, P. (2003), "Les Petits Sauvages: The Children of Eighteenth-Century New France", in N. Janovicek and J. Parr (eds.), *Histories of Canadian Children and Youth*, Oxford University Press, Toronto.

Neatby, H. (1953), *So Little for the Mind*, Clark Irwin, Toronto.

Osborne, K. (1996), "Education is the Best National Insurance: Citizenship Education in Canadian Schools, Past and Present", *Canadian and International Education/Éducation Canadienne et Internationale*, Vol. 25, No. 2, pp. 31-58.

Pacom, D. (2001), "Beyond Positivism: A Theoretical Evaluation of the Sociology of Youth", in M. Gauthier and D. Pacom (eds.), *Spotlight on Canadian Youth Research*, Les Presses de l'Université Laval, Sainte-Foy, Québec.

Piaget, J. (1957), "The Child and Modern Physics", *Scientific American*, Vol. 197, pp. 46-51.

Pollard, J. (2003), "A Most Remarkable Phenomenon: Growing up Métis: Fur Traders' Children in the Pacific Northwest", in N. Janovicek and J. Parr (eds.), *Histories of Canadian Children and Youth*, Oxford University Press, Toronto.

Rooke, P. and R.L. Schnell (1982), "Guttersnipes and Charity Children: Nineteenth Century Child Rescue in the Atlantic Provinces", in R.L. Schnell and P. Rooke (eds.), *Studies in Childhood History, A Canadian Perspective*, Detsileg Enterprises Ltd., Calgary, pp. 82-104.

Rooke, P. and R.L. Schnell (1983), "Discarding the Asylum", in P. Rooke, and R.L. Schnell (eds.), *From Child Rescue to the Welfare State in English-Canada, 1800-1950*, University Press of America, Lanham, MD.

Sadowski, M. (2003), *Adolescents at School: Perspectives on Youth, Identity, and Education*, Harvard University Press, Cambridge, MA.

Schissel, B. (1997), *Blaming Children: Youth Crime, Moral Panics and the Politics of Hate*, Fernwood Publishing, Halifax.

Schissel, B. (in Press), "Justice Undone: Public Panic, and the Condemnation of Children and Youth", in C. Krinsky (ed.), *The Sky is Falling: International Perspectives on Moral Panics*, Columbia University Press, Columbia.

Strong-Boag, V. (2002), "Getting to Now: Children in Distress in Canada's Past", in B. Wharf (ed.), *Community Work in Child Welfare*, Broadview Press, Toronto.

Sutherland, N. (2000), *Children in English-Canadian Society: Framing the Twentieth-Century Consensus*, Wilfred Laurier University Press, Waterloo.

Sutherland, N. (2002), *Growing Up: Childhood in English Canada from the Great War to the Age of Transition*, University of Toronto Press, Toronto.

Chapter 5
Policy-making to Promote Personalised Learning

by

Jean-Claude Ruano-Borbalan[*]

Ruano-Borbalan traces the history of ideas and knowledge about learning to discuss the issue of "personalization" with particular reference to France. An original characteristic of recent centuries, he argues, has been the development of massive systems to codify and reproduce society and a marked feature of such systems has been the form of their schools, classes and lessons. This is "efficient" when it comes to social reproduction and socialisation into society's values but not in terms of knowledge acquisition, learning capacity, and autonomy. Because every human story is different, learning reflexes cannot be dictated, in any case not by policy makers. But we can make a variety of activities and knowledge available to learners, in a range of educational situations and then let them decide "on their own", according to their preferences and personalities, how to progress and learn.

The context and challenge of the personalisation agenda

The energy that contemporary societies devote to educating and training the population is considerable. An original characteristic of recent centuries has been the development of massive systems to codify and organise forms and reproduce society. In OECD countries, these education and training systems absorb between a fifth and a quarter of central government funds as well as a notable share of corporate turnover, apart from what individuals and families provide in terms of financial and in-kind contributions. Dating back to the Renaissance, this form has helped shape civil society and the nation state. It is historically linked to the "classic" culture forged by the

---

[*] Director of Institut Demos, Paris, and formerly, the Director of Publication and Co-Editor-in-Chief of the journal *Sciences Humaines*.

governing classes. This culture became ossified in the 19th and 20th centuries and has remained – to the point of caricature in some countries like France – the prestigious inspiration of the entire initial education system and even adult learning, at least on the more general courses.

Since the 19th century, a marked feature of these systems has been the form of their schools, classes and lessons. Western-style education, which has now spread throughout the world, is characterised by the four "ones": one teacher, one class, one lesson and one subject. Teaching content is ultimately determined by two imperatives – academically-defined knowledge based on research, and general civic knowledge required of citizens in society. This system is widespread and "efficient" when it comes to social reproduction and socialisation into the standards and values laid down by the evolving state *i.e.* the common culture. However, this system is flawed in ways familiar to education scientists almost since the time of Rousseau as well as, of course, to students – it does not work efficiently for everyone in terms of knowledge acquisition, learning capacity, and autonomy.

Millions of pupils across the globe are learning but the returns to education can be extraordinarily low. In France, for instance, more than 100 000 teachers try to inculcate the rudiments of English, "the language of Shakespeare", but to little avail. The country's elite may be proficient in the international language but this is helped considerably by much determination and financial effort by their families. If change is taking place in this regard, my hypothesis would be (the situation is not well understood due to lack of relevant research) that it is because of society and individuals themselves, not because of efficient education content and methods being used to teach the language.

There is nothing new in noting this. The novelty may lie instead in that government circles have been won over by a new belief, developed and disseminated by academic economists for some forty years and relayed by the institutions of international co-operation. It holds that the main factor behind economic growth stems from the quality and productivity of our education systems.[1] In this context, David Miliband (Chapter 1) has endeavoured to show how crucial innovation is in the field of personalised learning for today's social and education systems. Without actually quoting them, he drew inspiration from the work of social thinkers and philosophers

---

[1] The fact that this is a "belief" does not mean that it is wrong: we all believe that the earth is a sphere measuring 40 000 km in circumference, revolving around the sun and maintained in orbit by the force of gravity. Admittedly we have no proof of this, and we base our belief on our trust in science which has developed the theory and confirmed it by analogy or deduction. The same goes for the economic theories now prevailing in international organisations.

like Jurgen Habermas, Ulrich Beck and, of course, Anthony Giddens on the subject of reflexive society and democratic space. He concludes that learners should be put "at the heart of the education system".

To this continental listener at the seminar, "putting learners at the heart of the system" sounded strangely dated. It was a goal of France's political and trade-union left-wing in the 1980s, and became the core concept of France's 1989 Education Act, initiated by Lionel Jospin who was later to become the socialist Prime Minister. Such determination to put learners at the centre of the system flopped in the land of Zinedine Zidane and Voltaire. France's 1989 Education Act was a final blow in the age-old battle waged by the "*école nouvelle*" or "new education" movement, the powerful French teaching unions, and the Left in general – and it was its swan song. After 1989, the emphasis switched to learning, discipline, combating violence in schools, values (including the debate on Muslim headscarves in schools, which remains so incomprehensible to many outside France), and school performance – all of which have preoccupied governments, education authorities and the general public alike.

Genuine concern with educational innovation and differentiated or personalised learning dates back to a previous era, and the Act marked the arrival in office of a small proportion of teachers who had advocated the concept in schools twenty years earlier. Broadly, the idea of personalised learning and similar educational innovations emerged in experiments in the 1970s. But it lost ground in the 1980s, even though its advocates came to power and wrote it into the Education Act, and it has virtually disappeared since. To put this in context, in France as in other OECD countries, societal change – the decline in educational institutions, individualism and changing parent-child relations – has altered relationships within schools and the classroom.

In terms of social doctrine and educational debate, however, the case appears to be clear, as highlighted in a recent report by the French *Commission du débat national sur l'avenir de l'école* (Commission for the National Debate on the Future of Education), which mobilised input from over a million people from September 2003 to March 2004. In nearly 600 pages, only seven of them address the issue of "pupil heterogeneity" encountered by lower secondary teachers in delivering the same basic curriculum to all children uniformly. The report's emphasis is on the system, education and the need to ensure attainment in the institutional and educational context as it stands, rather than on adaptation or personalisation. The very words "learner", "educational innovation" and "personalised learning" are scarcely to be found. In short, there has been a return to a classic approach to knowledge and learning, whereby teachers and schools transmit knowledge and ensure that it is learnt.

Education policy convergence

I was thus curious at the seminar to listen to a minister winning round a room of education officers with a discourse that economists believe to be innovative but which is familiar to French educational scientists and regarded as institutionally outmoded. It is tempting to believe that the French education system, archetypically centralised, is and will remain unique, with institutions and an ideological and educational rationale all of its own: but, this would be too simple. For, in every area of governance, OECD member countries are converging and, despite profound disparities, are eventually adopting similar evaluation and operating criteria. To be sure, my country is centralised, with a uniform curriculum and a discourse on the broad civic role played by school and education that sets it apart from Northern European or American systems. But in practice, it has just as many different forms of educational innovation and learning situation. And, over the past twenty years decentralised systems have also shifted towards standard-setting for individual subjects and general knowledge. The institutional outcome has been a narrowing of the gap between systems, particularly with regard to how schools operate. Whether decentralised or not, education systems are converging and governments are using similar rationales to justify very similar policies.

Crucially however, despite policy convergence and common goals, policy performance has been disappointing – everywhere. Why? Part of the answer may be found in a recent comparative micro-social study by the Belgian researcher Sabine Kahn (2003) on school reform in Belgium and Quebec. It highlights institutional and human resistance to any attempt at enhancing individual learning to improve the way education systems function. Specifically, the Belgian and Quebec reforms are worthwhile measures seeking high attainment for all and are doing away with *redoublement* (repeating a year). In both cases, says Kahn, it is a question of accepting that pupils are different and practising a form of education that takes those differences into account. A related aim – as it has long been throughout the OECD area – is for assessment to be formative rather than summative. Yet the evidence from the schools and primary classes in the study shows that ultimately teacher commitment and understanding are crucial when introducing new learning systems.

Take the example of *redoublement*, which has long been known to have stigmatising and harmful long-term consequences. Sabine Kahn points out that a majority of teachers – unlike the advocates of reform – are still in favour of this practice. Teachers possess representations and behavioural and cognitive routines which impede the introduction of learning situations that foster pupil autonomy. Such routines are also seen by the teachers as the expression of sound common sense. They know that the traditional form of classroom teaching is and will remain an appropriate response to the perhaps leading function of the education system, namely social and professional selection. It is not the sole aim of education to foster the development of every human being. While this utopian vision expresses a sound liberal principle, it clashes not only with the philosophical and political imperative of democratisation but also with the reality of professional and social selection, which is one of the key functions of education. Most teachers, pupils and parents believe that the traditional structure of classroom teaching, however archaic and difficult it may be, should not be called into question.

Human learning occurs at many levels

And so the question remains: given these constraints, and going beyond the discourse of certain economists, political analysts and politicians, how can we promote personalised learning at school? How can we enable children to learn? How can we ensure that, educational realities being what they are, individuals can enhance their innovative potential? After all, they are the ones doing the learning, and no educational programme or forecast can predict the unique path than a person will take towards (or away from) knowledge and learning. Because every human story is different, learning reflexes cannot be dictated, in any case not by policy makers. What we can do, as educationalists and psychologists have long maintained, is make a variety of activities and knowledge available to learners, in a range of educational situations. We can then let them decide "on their own", according to their preferences and personalities, how to progress and learn. No one can be forced to do this, but fortunately people are social animals, driven by an irrepressible need to discover and learn.

This is not a case of wishful thinking about how the education and training system, as an integral part of society at large, can be radically and definitively reformed and transformed to foster autonomous education and learning. Such a vision would make no sense. What does make sense is the observation that society has reached a "second modernity" – to use a term coined by the sociologist Anthony Giddens (1990, 1991) – a gap between the dominant form of authority and knowledge transmission in the school system, on the one hand, and the scope for individuals to act and reflect, on the other. For societies on the cutting edge of technology, co-operation, networking and free, personalised learning are both prerequisites and imperatives for political, economic and social development.

Although the focus here has been on human learning and on how it can be promoted and enhanced, other aspects of and requirements for such learning also need to be highlighted. Apart from the mechanisms and conditions for cognitive development, there are two further issues, the first being the nature of knowledge and learning, and the second the role of learning groups and educational mediators (*e.g.* teachers and educators). Knowledge and content are burning issues, though expressed differently in different countries and levels of education. Subject-specific didactics, types of knowledge, know-how and inter-personal skills, together with self-teaching and on-line training using new information and communication technologies, figure prominently in education debates. Research into learning has focused heavily on the ownership of knowledge by learners. Debates recognise the importance of what people should be able to do rather than merely what education and training institutions and the business world require of them. Such discussion has shown how useful it is to link the social dimension to the purely cognitive aspects of acquiring knowledge and skills.

In this respect, consideration of how to use technology in education and especially for distance learning has been fruitful, illusions about its potential notwithstanding. It has raised the issue of self-teaching which the new communication tools were aimed to promote, and has questioned the traditional structure of education, the role of educators and teachers, and specific issues relating to knowledge acquisition by learners (such as motivation when alone, forms of navigation and course). Though not necessarily intended to replace traditional forms, the new modes of learning and education, often devised from necessity such as physical distance, are valuable test-beds for innovation. They are not the only ones: teachers in charge of students with various forms of disability have also had to introduce personalised forms of learning. It would be wise to look carefully at these experiences and innovations to gain insights into what could be transferable to mainstream teaching.

Finally, there is the role of teaching specialists and learner groups. Learning is a personal process but it requires the assistance of an educator to facilitate acquisition and mediate between the knowledge passed to, and that built up by, the learner. Hence, the role of educators and their pedagogical and subject-specific skills are central issues to be debated – the role of educators and their style of teaching, their motivation and energy, the physical resources at their disposal and their teaching methods, including how they relate to the socio-cultural profile of their pupils. Only the learner's own cognitive characteristics are more important in explaining learning outcomes.

Social psychology and the analysis of learning groups remind us of how closely interlinked are all the players involved. The presence of others and social interplay are – as in many social situations – powerful motivations for action and learning. Three propositions are central to personalised learning and should help guide consideration of pedagogical and didactic approaches which include some element of self-instruction along with proposed educational activities and content:

- First, learning is a complex individual process, contingent on the identity of the learner who controls the pace of his/her learning and motivation.

- Second, people learn better in a co-operative environment together with their peers.

- Third, people would not know what to learn if educators/mediators were not there to help introduce them to what or how to learn.

An outstanding question then is how to promote proposals with the many different institutions and players involved when they enjoy a large degree of autonomy. An initial answer could be the production and dissemination of substantiated knowledge on the mechanisms of human learning – there is clear need for a resource centre on recognised knowledge and skills in the field of human learning. The first and most pressing step is to construct a system for observing, discussing and defining academic knowledge. This is no simple undertaking, of course, and would go beyond anything so far attempted or experimented within any country. Barriers to doing so stem largely from the ideologies and cultures prevailing in the administrative and political machinery. But they are also inherent to the fields of psychology, social science and educational practice in which symbolic and academic hierarchies and the frontiers of knowledge create divides that prevent much-needed communication between the different actors involved.

This suggests the solution of an international think-tank on human learning. Its remit might cover: first, mapping areas where the knowledge base is already robust (and we do know a considerable amount); second, analysing key areas that are still at issue and pose problems; and third identifying uncharted areas that require research. Such a think-tank should work in a broad field covering not only the socio-institutional aspects of the external learning environment and the psychological aspects of motivation and "internal" constraints, but also adult education, early childhood education, pedagogy, learning methods, and cognitive psychology pertaining to knowledge. To enhance the learning environment and hence individual differentiation or personalised learning will require such an effort and we otherwise risk being stuck with amnesia and inertia. An institutional instrument for the evaluation, elaboration and dissemination of academic research and knowledge on learning and education is crucial. It should be international and could be of assistance to a wide variety of those engaged in education, *e.g.* families, pupils, teachers, school heads and administrators, encouraging them towards a change in practice, gradually perhaps but in a sustainable way.

References

Giddens, A. (1990), *The Consequences of Modernity*, Stanford University Press, Stanford.

Giddens, A. (1991), *Modernity and Self-identity*, Stanford University Press, Stanford.

Kahn, S., B. Rey, V. Carette and A. Defrance (2003), *Les compétences à l'école. Apprentissage et évaluation*, De Boeck.

Chapter 6
Personalised Learning 2025

by
Johan Peter Paludan[*]

This chapter examines the elements that might lead the educational systems towards greater personalisation, namely, attitudes, motivation, the needs of society, and technological possibilities. It then considers how key stakeholders – students, teachers, parents, the labour market, society – might react. The preliminary conclusion is that personalisation will emerge but the ways it will come about are open to debate, and four scenarios present different options: 1) total personalisation; 2) personalised timing; 3) automated teaching; 4) the status quo. Personalised education will not be possible without simultaneously improving the productivity of the system and it may also mean that it becomes more difficult to ascertain what individual students have gained from their studies and more discontinuous education may have negative effects on society's cohesiveness. Personalisation characterised by easing the individual student's passage through the system will be much less controversial than one that also personalises educational content.

Why has personalised learning not advanced further?

There is something both politically correct and inherently redundant about the concept of "personalised learning" in the sense that it would be strange to meet anyone who was opposed to it. It is in the spirit of the times that it seems superfluous to attach the label "personalised" before "education". And yet, we also know that the reality is far removed from the ideal. Although students no longer recite their lessons in chorus as they did a

---

[*] Director of the Copenhagen Institute for Futures Studies, Denmark.

century ago, we are still a long way from a truly personalised educational system. There are several possible reasons for this.

The educational sector would probably point to a lack of resources as the prime reason why personalisation has not advanced further. Yet the problem here is that there is no natural limit on spending, as education is a form of maximisation not optimisation demand. An example of an optimisation demand is when you are hungry: your condition improves as you begin to eat but eventually you reach a point at which your need has been met and any further eating is bad for you. In contrast, maximisation needs have no natural satisfaction point: the more resources are allocated, the better. Education and health care are classic maximisation demands in that there are always needs which have not been covered and which argue for further resources. The English might be ready to describe someone as "too clever by half", but this is not really possible and one can never learn too much. This is one reason why society has an ambivalent attitude towards the educational sector. We know that we cannot do without it but we also know that it can use up all available resources and still look around hungrily for more. Hence society – or rather the authorities whose job it is to allocate resources – must always be on guard lest education grows beyond all limits.

An equally important reason for the discrepancy between the professed ideals for the educational system and actual conditions is the institutionalised conservatism that suffuses any system. Those who run it – the teachers – are older than those who use the system – the students. It is true that the education system is not the only one marked by rigidities; most institutions have a tendency to cater to the needs of the past. But unlike other institutions, we have all had relationships with education and come away with an emotionally charged attitude towards it. Although not all share a positive, nostalgic attitude, this is the prevalent sentiment; the human mind has a remarkable ability to let the passage of time draw a conciliatory veil over something that may not really have been that much fun at the time.

A third factor restraining the evolution of the educational system is the process, related to nostalgia, that makes adults feel that in order for the younger generation to develop into sterling human beings, it must go through a process that is a faithful copy of the regime that the older generation went through. Hence every time the educational system is revised up goes the cry "*o tempora, o mores*".

The purpose of this chapter is to examine the prospects of personalised education system in the year 2025. Over the course of such a long span of time, radical changes are possible but we should not underestimate the inertia inherent in the present educational system. Nor should we over-estimate the societal impact of changing the educational system for the rate of change of society, coupled with developing lifelong learning, means that the established educational system no longer has the monopoly on imparting skills and knowledge (though it is where the groundwork for lifelong learning is laid). On the other hand, the concept of lifelong learning as such implies a personalisation of learning. The increasing amount of learning conducted after the end of formalised education does not usually take place in classrooms and the learner often chooses the subject matter.

The future

The educational system is one of the most forward-looking of any. One attends school for the sake of future gain rather than immediate gratification. As Seneca wrote, '*Non scholae, sed vitae discimus*' (we learn not for school but for life). But, it is necessary to emphasise in this connection that the future does not yet exist, which we should bear in mind considering how various kinds of mysticism (such as astrology, numerology, etc.) flourish. We all live in the Now with some idea of where we came from – the Past – and some notions of where we are heading, the Future.

It might be tempting to disregard the future altogether since it does not exist and one cannot "go on a field trip to study it". But that would be just as wrong as believing that the future already exists. Decisions that will affect the future must be made today, however difficult that future may be to grasp, and we all have expectations of how the future will turn out, some conscious and others unconscious. (Conscious expectations are the easier to live with as they enable us at the least to realise when we were wrong – a qualified, conscious guess being thus better than an unconscious expectation.) The importance of considering the future applies even more forcefully when shaping the educational system as it "manufactures goods" which have to last for at least 60 to 80 years or perhaps longer still, considering the prospects of further increases in the human lifespan.

This chapter does not examine every aspect of the educational system but rather the possibilities for it to become more personalised, coming back to the gulf to be narrowed between the current educational ideal – personalisation – and the existing conditions within the system. It examines the elements that might lead the educational systems towards greater personalisation and then considers who the stakeholders are in the educational system and their interest in having a more personalised system. This discussion is put into a broader perspective through scenarios to examine the prospects for a more personalised educational system.

A number of elements work towards a more personalised educational system, namely, attitudes to people, motivation, the needs of society, and technological possibilities. Most of these elements have been around for a long time, but have not had decisive effects on current educational systems, given inertia and conservatism. Present inertia does not necessarily mean that the future will be the same as these factors may enjoy greater effect between now and 2025.

Personalised learning and people

People differ. When children begin school, girls are already generally more mature than boys and this only corrects itself later on. Despite awareness of this disparity, the normal practise is still to lump children together by date of birth at the beginning stages of the educational system. Conformity has a long history. Marxist theory would suggest that the explanation for conformity lies in material factors: societies where hunger and want are facts of life develop norms for acceptable behaviour and are not tolerant of those who depart from them, since the risks of non-conformity appear too large. When society has a low rate of change, as in many cases historically, it is based on experience. Older people are "smarter" because it takes time to gather experience and hence they (including the teachers) have authority.

Modern society is undergoing rapid changes and with it authority. One possible reason for the education's resistance to change is that going from a society of authority based on societal position to one where authority must constantly be earned increases the demands on the system itself. It also argues for the replacement of an entire generation of teachers who are too old to be taught new tricks. The industrialised society may be behind us, but the educational system has not yet realised this. Industrialised society was governed by an engineering logic – standardised, measurable, and time-conscious. This logic makes it perfectly reasonable to group students by year of birth and for the educational system to produce standardised "goods" that can be classified into first-rate, second-rate, etc., based on an objective system of evaluation. One such way to measure is in units of time, and probably no modern organisation bases its activities more on time than educational institutions. In the labour market, on the other hand, the continual automation of production and global outsourcing mean that an ever increasing segment of the labour force goes from having specific work hours to having tasks to complete. In schools, industrial time-based lessons are still paramount.

Therefore, the first step towards creating a genuinely personalised educational system is to realise that the industrial society is no longer with us.

Personalised learning and motivation

The next step is for the educational system to recognise that the conditions for motivation have changed. The use of physical punishment within the educational system has abated but it has not been too many years since it was in regular use nor did the English boarding schools have a monopoly on the more brutal forms of educational motivation. But the essential qualities that a modern educational system seeks to develop in students cannot be imparted through threats quite apart from any purely humanitarian arguments. Rote learning may be enough to knock ready knowledge into students but the qualities demanded by the knowledge society have to be enticing enough that the students want to learn them.

Lars Henrik Schmidt (1999) has analysed how education changes as we move from a traditional society to a modern society. Originally the purpose of education was to convey knowledge from one person to another. The learned transmitted their knowledge to the ignorant who, with really close attention, may hope to become almost as knowledgeable in time. Physical motivation was thought a suitable means of inducing the ignorant to pay attention, which might be described as "gas tank education" as it sees the students as empty vessels to be filled up. In time it became the purpose of the educational system to impart "qualifications", so that it became the market, especially for labour, which determines whether a qualification is worth anything, not teachers. Today this process has reached a point where among the most important qualities are "competencies" – unique, personal characteristics such as creativity, a sense of humour, and the like. Obviously an educational process that is supposed to foster the unique competencies of each individual student cannot use the same motivational means as one based on rote learning.

One of the ways to make education more enticing is to tailor it more to individual students. If they feel that the system respects them and takes their individuality into account, they are more disposed to make an effort. This needs not mean ending up with an educational system where every student sits in splendid isolation with their own personalised course. Humans are social animals, young people not the least who are most likely to say "to meet others" in answer to the question about why they go to school. Nor does it imply an educational system where the students can choose independently what they want to learn. The notion of being responsible for one's own learning, a watchword in parts of the pedagogic establishment, is nonsense at the level of primary and secondary education when students lack the basis for exercising such responsibility.

Personalised learning and society

The needs of society will be determined by the evolution of a knowledge society. The sum total of accumulated knowledge continues to grow at a prodigious rate and has led Anthony Giddens to refer to the "reflexive society" where the more that is known, the more that knowledge acquires an independent effect on developments. More negative reasons for the transition are global patterns of labour, where the outsourcing of simpler tasks to other countries – currently China and India are favourite destinations – means that more complex, knowledge-intensive ones play an increasing role in the economies of OECD countries. One characteristic of the knowledge society is organisational structures that are far more decentralised than before. The rigid hierarchies of the industrial society are replaced by looser, network-like organisational structures. Knowledge-intensive tasks require independence, commitment, and the responsibility of the individual employee. The business community will increasingly want the educational system to produce those qualities, which cannot be forced; they have to be fostered through a more personalised educational system.

Many years ago the Norwegian criminologist Nils Christie (1970) published a book with the fascinating title *Hvis skolen ikke fandtes* (If there were no School). Fortunately for the educational sector, his conclusion was that if school didn't exist then it would be necessary to invent it. He pointed out that if the purpose of the educational system was only to provide young people with the ability to read, write, and count, then it could be done in considerably shorter time than is actually the case. If you personalised entry to education – that is, let the students start when they were mature enough and motivated to learn – you could shorten the educational process considerably. According to Christie, the reason for the increase of the educational cycle from 6-7 years (and that only patchily observed in the Danish countryside so that the children could help with the farming) to 9 or 10 to 12 years is that the school has a purpose beyond that of teaching skills. It inculcates specific attitudes.

This development can be linked to the whole "outsourcing" of functions that used to belong to the family/household including rearing the next generation to either the private or the public sector. A major factor in this development is the higher incidence of women in the workplace, which is where the school has to step in. The result is a democratisation of the system. When in earlier times it was only the upper class that sent their children to boarding school and turned over child-rearing to others, today this phenomenon has spread to the rest of the population with both parents in the labour force and leaving more functions, including the shaping of attitudes, to the school. In modern societies with decentralised tasks, individual attitudes have also become more important. As employees become their own supervisors, their mental status as individuals also becomes more important. The lengthening of the educational process is a symptom of the growing importance of the attitude-shaping function and this is unlikely to diminish in the future. The attitudes that the educational system is expected to foster do not thrive on "job lot education". More personalised solutions are required.

Personalised learning and technology

The implications of the attitude-shaping function illustrate the insatiability of the educational sector. Since resources always will be limited, an increase in educational productivity is required. But as Jean-Claude Ruano-Borbalan (Chapter 5) and others have pointed out, the returns for the educational sector are just not good enough. There is no established tradition in education of thinking actively about increased productivity – the negative effects of cutbacks are well-known but specific efforts to increase productivity are rare. I would maintain that it is impossible to create a more personalised educational system without productivity increases.

As seen in other sectors, productivity can be increased through the use of technology, which can automate simpler tasks and spare the more expensive production elements – humans – for those tasks for which they are indispensable. Technology usually begins as scarce and expensive but then becomes established and cheaper, while the price associated with people does not diminish. As information technology becomes more mature, it should by 2025 and through the use of interactive systems contribute to increased productivity in the education sector. This would make room for more personalised education.

One of the most personalised forms of education is the tutorial, where intense student-teacher interaction permits the thorough exploration of subjects. If we wish to approach this ideal, then technology must take on as much of the work as possible. It is only our imagination that limits the ways it can be put to use – not the hardware but the software. The educational sector needs to invest in the development of software. The problem is circular: the educational sector has no tradition of thinking of technological solutions while detailed knowledge of conditions in education is a prerequisite for the development of technological solutions for it.

While there are many reasons to expect or advocate the shift towards a more personalised educational system, important question concern how this might come about. The discussion of information technology highlights one crucial prerequisite for a more personalised education system. Another important prerequisite is that those who use or influence the system have a vested interest in promoting such a development. It is therefore necessary to address stakeholder interests.

Stakeholders

Students

It is only a slight overstatement to say that the main interest of the students is to have fun. They may from time to time consider the importance of learning something, but that is mostly taken for granted. When one is forced to go to school, as is usually the case in a modern society, the learning becomes less important – to the students if not to the parents – and the main preoccupation is to make the place you are obliged to attend as tolerable as possible. As stated in the words of the pop song some years ago: "All I wanna do, is have some fun, I got a feeling, I'm not the only one."

There is a parallel between the school situation and the ideas that the Copenhagen Institute for Futures Studies have generated concerning developments in the labour market. The continual automation of routine tasks means that those tasks that can be measured by the clock are disappearing while those tasks defined by their content and by deadlines are growing, both relatively and absolutely. Work becomes more and more "hard fun". It is "fun" because the work becomes more interesting. It is "hard" because deadlines promote stress and because the task has no natural limit other than the deadline itself – the work can always be improved upon. And it is "hard" because the work to a growing extent falls to the individual who is personally responsible for managing time and keeping to the deadline. More than almost anything else in the world, education is still defined by units of time, with classes defined by year of birth, fixed time tables, terms, and examinations of fixed lengths. Turning away from this fixation with time may be one way to personalise learning in the future.

Applying the concept of "hard fun" to education leads to the question of how to increase the element of fun ("edutainment"?). A dedicated teacher with a powerful personality can make learning engaging, but that kind of teacher will always be in short supply. Until now, the school has overcome its lack of entertainment value by a mixture of coercion and playing to the social needs of young people, but in the future it will be necessary to turn to information technology and more personalised teaching to secure a continued interest in learning.

The use of information technology as an educational tool is still in its infancy, but considering the ease with which children are able to master video games – without reading the manuals – this gives an inkling of what an enormous educational potential IT has. One of at least two reasons why it is so easy for children to learn video games: they think it is fun and they get immediate feedback. The second reason raises one of the most powerful educational principle – the need for an immediate response informing students whether they are on the right track or not. This is the reason why some, do much better at oral exams than written ones as the observant candidate constantly receives information from the examiner's body language and can tell if it is time to think of something else. In earlier times, the privileged classes could hire private tutors to expose their children to this educational method. In the future, information technology will have to take over the role of private tutor.

In some fields, the effectiveness of information technology as an educational tool has already been demonstrated. The military has experimented with technology and found that IT-based teaching can help ensure that each student has learned what is needed. Control points in the programme stop the student unless mastery has been demonstrated, which is a more effective way to control the learning process than either oral or written exams. It is also quite possible that IT-based teaching can make it fun to learn subjects that not even the most dedicated teacher can make interesting. Back in the days when mass education was in its infancy, the school was often the first place you got your hands on a book. It is strange that today the school is not the place the young person goes to in order to find IT.

The use of information technology can contribute to a personalisation of teaching methods. By developing programmes that are designed to differentiate between their users, products can fit individual requirements far better than any book and relieve the teacher of much of the routine work, so freeing up time to spend with the individual student. If the year of birth is abandoned as the criterion for starting in school in favour of a more personalised evaluation, even classroom teaching may become far more personalised than it is today. Finally, the development of educational methods that are more "hard fun" could contribute to solving the problem of reconciling students' desire for having fun with the interest of the rest of society who want the student to learn something useful.

Teachers

What might be the future interests of teachers? The straightforward answer is "meaningful work and better pay". But if learning is personalised in the coming years as this paper proposes, and if that personalisation process is carried out through a more extensive use of technology, it must be expected that many teachers will not be able to see the advantages. Personalisation and an increased use of technology imply quite a change for teachers' work. Those who have been teaching for many years are likely to have fixed ideas about how things should be done, which may prevent them from appreciating the advantages of new methods. The age profile of teachers is thus crucial to responses to the concept of a personalised learning system. This profile varies from country to country. In Denmark the age profile of teachers represents quite a challenge as a very large group of teachers from both primary and secondary schools will retire in the next 5 to 10 years. To replace these teachers will itself be a big task. That is the downside. The upside is that this opens up the possibility of a fresh start.

The odds of the teacher's role becoming more meaningful are likely in the long run. If machines can take care of most routine work, the more interesting parts of teaching will come to dominate. The prospect of better pay is quite another issue, despite their salaries being pretty low considering their educational background and the enormous responsibility they bear. Perhaps they will just need to accept the saying: 'Work carries its own reward'.

Parents

Over the last century, modern society has changed from one where children were a burden on the poor to one where children are a luxury of the rich. Fertility has plummeted to below the replacement level in practically every OECD country. If fertility levels stay as low as they currently are, the populations of the rich countries will eventually die out, though of course this is unlikely to happen as these countries can remedy their declining populations by increasing immigration, or else these levels could rise again. There are understandable reasons for the low fertility levels: better contraception, the increased participation of women in the labour market, the rising age at which mothers have their first child, and, last but not least, the ever-increasing social demands that turn children into increasingly longer and more expensive projects. There has been radical change from a situation in centuries past where children were put to work before age 10 years to one where many turn 30 before they can stand entirely on their own feet. Some, indeed, never get to stand on their own feet!

If fertility levels will remain low, a child's best chance of having siblings is for the parents to divorce and remarry. Ordinarily parents care for all their children and see them as individuals, but there is obviously a big difference between having a whole flock of children and having only one. Maybe the behaviour of today's youth is, in part, a reaction to the pressure caused by inflated parental expectations. Parents who have only one or two children will regard them more as unique individuals and it will seem natural to them that they want their education to be tailored to the child's wishes and abilities. Parents are thus an important force making education more personalised and will demand it as they realise that one cannot learn too much and perceive personalised learning as a better way to teach than more traditional educational methods.

These wishes must, however, be considered in conjunction with other desires that parents may have towards education. The more that dual-career households become the norm, the more the school will be perceived as a place to care for and bring up children. Parents will increasingly feel that the school must take a greater role in child rearing, perhaps with their children's classmates as at least as important to their development as the parents. This used to be the province of the upper classes sending their children to the "right" boarding school, but as this desire spreads, society may run into considerable trouble accommodating parental wishes to have their children associate with the "right" classmates. Who will go to school with those children the others deem unacceptable?

But the greatest challenge to a more personalised education system may well be that the more differentiated the teaching becomes, the less one can be sure that the student actually learns what is needed in order to succeed in later life. The problem will be to how to declare the "content" of a personalised educational programme in a way that reassures demanding parents.

The labour market

While it is a massive simplification to address the labour market as a single entity, there are some likely general tendencies that are interesting to confront with a more personalised educational system. A growing part of the labour market will see one's educational background as an "admission ticket" – proof that you have gone through a process that demonstrates general abilities on which a further part of your lifelong learning can build. It has come to the point where no formal qualifications will by themselves be sufficient. This applies even to the health care sector that may still require specific qualifications. All new employees will to some degree be trained to hold down any given job. The continuing move towards the knowledge society also leads to the automation of routine functions and an increase in those who require an independent, creative effort.

For the labour market a more personalised education system has its advantages and disadvantages. There will not be the same need for unskilled labour in the future, so it benefits the labour market if personalised learning encourages the student to study harder. It likewise benefits the labour market if personalised learning fosters the personal competencies to handle creative tasks. The major disadvantage is that a more personalised educational path will be more difficult for the labour market to evaluate. It will be more difficult to determine if an applicant has the necessary basic and general qualifications needed for a career of lifelong learning. This may lead the labour market to set up its own accrediting bodies to compensate for the diffuse qualifications that applicants of the future will present from their education.

Society

It is even more of a simplification to speak of the interests of "society" as a stakeholder in the educational system but as it is society that largely finances and regulates the educational system, its ability to influence the system is considerable. Daniel Patrick Moynihan's reflection is pertinent here:

> "The central conservative truth is that it is culture, not politics, which determines the success of a society. The central liberal truth is that politics can change a culture and save it from itself."

This highlights the school's central position in society as arguably the most important tool for maintaining or changing the existing culture. This is why school attendance is mandatory in most societies – society making sure that all its members have undergone the same cultural "training".

There are many definitions of culture. One is that culture is habits – internalised values that govern the choices people make. It is culture that shapes a society's identity as a society. There are many signs that modern societies lack the coherence that they used to have with increasing individualism and anti-authoritarian attitudes. So too does secularisation or, more precisely, the de-institutionalisation of religion. Religion is growing mostly outside the established, largely national, religious organisations. All this leads to a change from a well-defined hierarchical society with common values to what could be dubbed "the peripheral society" – a society with no clear focus.

Thus there is a latent conflict between a more personalised educational system and society's wish to maintain or change its culture. This suggests the need to distinguish between form and substance. An educational system that personalises the form – that allows the student to choose the schedule and the methodology – will cause much less concern than one that personalises the subjects that are taught. Indeed, personalisation of the educational form may well strengthen existing efforts to tighten up educational contents so that set canons and national curricula could get a new lease of life.

Scenarios

So far the focus has been the forces that might promote a more personalised education system and on how key stakeholders might react to such a system. The preliminary conclusion is that such a system will emerge: the desire exists and the means are available. But personalisation of learning can happen in many ways. The way it will come about and how fast it will happen are both open to debate.

One way to explore these questions is to use scenarios. At the Copenhagen Institute for Futures Studies, we like to use the "cross-division method". There are other ways to generate scenarios but this way is easy to grasp, methodologically and in terms of results. This method consists of examining the uncertain factors inherent in the problem under consideration and estimate which of these are both crucial to the problem and the most uncertain. The two most important factors can then be matched up and provide the basis to construct four scenarios.

Looking at personalised learning, one might focus on these following factors.

Framework

- *Economic growth*, which will primarily serve to regulate the speed of developments. High economic growth will facilitate the reorganisation of the educational sector, and may also lead to a development of the labour market, increasing the demand for more creative employees.

- *Culture*, where the extremes are *laissez-faire* and tight control. *Laissez-faire* would allow a total personalisation of both timing and content.

Process

- *Face-to-face or IT based?* This is a spurious distinction as both methods will probably be used, but one might wonder where the emphasis will lie. If the resources available for personalisation are sparse then it may be tempting to go with the "cheap", IT-based, automated solution.

- *Timing*: either focus on the maturity of the individual student or on the content of the education. Again it will most probably be a mix of both rather than one or the other. Nevertheless, an interesting question is whether future developments will be marked more by personalisation of timing or by personalisation of content.

Goals

- *Elite or equity?* Is the goal of the personalisation to help the best students or is it to make sure that everybody learns enough to get by?

- *Autonomy or community?* Is the goal to create strong individuals or to strengthen society?

- *Individual or labour market?* Is personalisation primarily to benefit the individual or the labour market?

Guidance

- *Controlled or "free fall"?* The latter refers to a rapid relaxation of official regulations concerning education. While the total removal of regulation seems unlikely, it is interesting to speculate how much the government will wish to steer the process of personalisation.

- *Run by students and parents or from above?* How much control will society relinquish?

- *Public or market?* If personalisation becomes widespread, one argument for a publicly run and all-inclusive educational system disappears, though it is still possible to have a publicly-financed system each individual can decide how and when to use. Bertel Haarder, the Danish Minister of Education in the 1980s, suggested that every citizen should receive an educational coupon book (entitlement), which some would take all of in a single stretch while others would spread it out and take it in smaller chunks over their whole life.

The above is merely indicative of the methodology, which can be further illustrated by selecting two dimensions to launch a sample scenario exercise. One obvious pairing would be economic growth (from high to low) and culture (from *laissez-faire* to tightening).

One does not have to be Marxist to say that the cultural dimension has a certain correlation with the economic. Low economic growth will probably heighten the popular perception of external threats, leading to an increased desire to strengthen national identity. Conversely, high growth could facilitate *laissez-faire* developments; not only will there be optimism but also the necessary surplus for the investments required by a personalised educational system. The cultural dimension also covers some of the other dimensions mentioned above. *Laissez-faire* is likely to co-exist with market-guidance, individual autonomy, and student/parent control. Cultural tightening, on the other hand, is more likely to co-exist with a publicly run system where the personalisation that might be promoted would be aimed to strengthen society and the labour market.

Combining the two dimensions gives the following four scenarios.

Scenario 1: total personalisation

A future marked by a high economic growth will encourage *laissez-faire* attitudes in all areas. It leads to the speedy integration of the EU despite its expansion. A "European" national identity is unlikely to have solidified by 2025, but it is on its way. There is more general acceptance of the process of globalisation. There is not only personalisation of each student's route through the educational system, but also of educational content. The labour market will probably create its own assessment system.

Scenario 2: personalised timing

A future marked by the combination of high growth and cultural tightening could come about if the continuing immigration to the industrialised countries fosters a sense that the national identity is endangered. This would create a strong desire for a national curriculum and a demand that it be followed for the student is to become a full-fledged member of society. Education will be perceived as a means of ensuring that the immigrants (who are necessary to accept whether because of international obligations or of the need for imported labour) will become "nationalised". The advantages of taking individual factors into consideration are recognised and the immigrants make these even clearer; they are of different ages and adult education is increasingly important. Hence, this scenario is characterised by the personalised timing of each student's journey through the educational system.

Scenario 3: automated teaching

Low economic growth highlights the importance of the productivity of the educational system; the more that IT can be used to shift from expensive teachers to cheap interactive systems, the better. Immigration has been brought under control and EU integration has been hampered by its expansion still further to the East. This and the low economic growth, due partly by outsourcing to other parts of the world, emphasise the value of a highly qualified labour force. Anything that might dampen student motivation to learn must be removed from the educational system, leading to the personalisation of content as well as timing.

Scenario 4: the status quo

A situation marked by low economic growth and a desire for cultural tightening might be described provocatively as "the status quo". Resources are not available for investments in the educational system and there is no desire for them either. Each national system feels threatened and has little appetite for experimentation.

These four scenario outlines are examples of how the future may be explored, including the future of personalised learning. This could become a vital aspect of the educational system, which is in turn a crucial part of modern society. An evaluation of future prospects is therefore a difficult and complex undertaking for which the scenario methodology is well suited.

Conclusion

There is a substantial divergence between what might be termed the "Zeitgeist" and the educational system. On the one hand, we live in societies characterised by increasing individualism, extolling the uniqueness of each person and promoting the notion that they should be able to exercise greater control over their own lives. Key events have been the fall of the Berlin Wall and the victory of market ideology. On the other hand, education systems still tend to have fixed content and timing. It seems likely that it will be the educational system that will have to adapt.

A key question is whether progress towards more personalised learning will be hampered by the insatiability of the educational system. Personalised education will not be possible without simultaneously improving the productivity of the system. Since this will require significant investments, all things being equal a high economic growth will encourage more personalisation. It is not, however, without its downsides. It becomes more difficult to ascertain what individual students have gained from their studies and concerns may grow that a more discontinuous education will undermine society's cohesiveness. Personalisation characterised by easing the individual student's passage through the system will therefore be much less controversial than one that also personalises educational content. Even so, considerable progress has already been made regarding personalisation of timing.

The basic challenge to education in modern societies is that the rest of society, especially the labour market, will demand that the system produces more and better qualified people. The continuing development within the global division of labour means that the OECD countries must continue along the road towards the knowledge society in order to maintain and increase their current standard of living. But people cannot be forced to be more and better qualified, they have to be coaxed. Everything else being equal, more personalised education will be more attractive than existing inflexible educational systems.

References

Christie, N. (1970), *Hvis skolen ikke fandtes*, Oslo/Copenhagen.

Giddens, A. (1990), *Runaway World*, London.

Guillou, J. (1981), *Ondskan*, Stockholm.

Huntington, S. (2000), "Cultures Count", in L. Harrison and S. Huntington (eds), *Culture Matters*, New York.

Jensen, R.(1999), *Dream Society*, New York.

Scherfig, H. (1940), *Det forsømte forår* (Misspent Spring), Copenhagen.

Schmidt, L. H. (1999) Diagnosis 1-111, Copenhagen.

Chapter 7
The Future of Public Services: Personalised Learning

by

Charles Leadbeater[*]

Charles Leadbeater argues that personalisation has the potential to reorganise the way public goods and services are created and delivered. Such reorganisation requires exploration of different approaches to personalisation and this chapter explores these: bespoke service, mass customisation, and mass-personalisation. Personalisation through participation allows users a more direct say in the way the service they use is designed, planned, delivered and evaluated. This involves the following steps: *intimate consultation*: *expanded choice*: *enhanced voice*: *partnership provision*: *advocacy*: *co-production*: *funding*. Personalised learning assumes that learners should be actively engaged in setting their own targets, devising their own learning plans and goals, choosing from among a range of different ways to learn. This implies far-reaching changes in the role of professionals and schools. But the biggest challenge is what it means for inequality: the more that services become personalised, the more that public resources will have to be skewed towards the least well-off.

Personalisation is a potent but highly contested idea that could be as influential as privatisation was in the 1980s and 1990s in reshaping public provision around the world. Privatisation started out as a Conservative policy in 1984, at the height of neo-liberalism but has since been widely adopted by governments around the world of different political persuasions. Personalisation could have a similar impact and reach because it could provide a new organising logic for public provision.

---

[*] An independent writer and adviser on innovation, entrepreneurship and the knowledge economy and a Senior Research Associate with the think-tank Demos (London).

Privatisation was a simple idea: putting public assets into private ownership would create more powerful incentives for managers to deliver greater efficiency and innovation. In reality, the conditions to make privatisation work are far more complex, including competitive markets and corporate cultures. Personalisation appears just as simple: by putting users at the heart of services, enabling them to become participants in the design and delivery, so services will be more effective by mobilising millions of people as co-producers of the public goods they value. Making personalisation a reality will be as complex and contingent as privatisation.

Personalisation has the potential to reorganise the way we create public goods and deliver public services. Yet unlocking that potential requires exploration of what personalisation could mean.

Approaches to personalisation

At the moment personalisation seems to mean providing better access and some limited say for users over how existing services are provided in largely traditional ways. This "shallow" personalisation offers modest customisation of mass-produced, standardised services to partially adapt them to user needs. "Deep" personalisation would give users a far greater role – and also far greater responsibilities – for designing solutions from the ground up. Personalisation could just mean more 24-7 call centres, booked appointments and timely access to standardised services or at the other extreme it could mean promoting greater capacity for self-management and self-organisation. Personalisation could be a sustaining innovation designed to make existing systems more personalised, or it could be a disruptive innovation designed to put the users in the driving seat as designers and paymasters of services. It could be a programme to apply a lick of new paint to fading public services, or it could be the harbinger of entirely new organisational logic. It is worth briefly exploring three different but potentially complementary ideas of personalised learning.

Bespoke service

The first is that personalised services are bespoke, tailored to the needs of individual clients. When we go to the hairdresser, the accountant or the psychoanalyst we get a personalised service, in the sense that the professional provider applies their knowledge to solve the clients' problems. In an ideal world, education should be like that. Learning is vital to who we are and what we become. It provides us with access to the knowledge, skills and crucially the cultural capital which give us our distinctive sense of ourselves. Creating a programme of learning for someone is not unlike the task of building a complex highly sensitive product like a Formula One racing car. What can we learn from that?

At the Formula One BAR racing team in the English Cotswolds, for example, the complexity of the task undertaken by the 400 staff is staggering. It takes 15 months to develop a racing car for a 16-week season. That means next season's car is already in development while the current car is being raced. And racing itself is a constant process of innovation and adaptation. A car is made up of about 3 000 components. Each of these will be redesigned three times in the course of a season. The BAR machine shop has to make 10 000 components and keep track of them. About 400 of these components need special attention because they are safety critical. After each outing they need to be tested for cracking or attrition. Each season the team makes 125 cars, each one slightly different from the other. Every week two or three cars are being tested as another is in development for the following season and another three will be on the way to a race. Racing, production and innovation are all rolled into a tightly knit, continuous process.

Coordinating such a complex process is a nightmare. Just keeping track of parts is difficult enough. The 25 section leaders used to meet two to three times a week, to make sure everyone was abreast of what was needed. The meetings used to last three hours and still they made mistakes. The process at BAR has become far more manageable, thanks to two changes to the process. First, they have installed a state-of-the-art information system which allows each part to be tracked through the system. Anyone can access the system. It is not actively coordinated from the centre; instead it operates according to a few simple rules: people making parts are expected to take responsibility for checking when they are needed rather than waiting to be told what to do. They have to respond to demand. The second ingredient is the team shares a simple purpose. Everyone working at BAR is passionate about racing. They are bonded together as a team. Simple rules, combined with a simple purpose (and good information), allow the horrendously complex mix of production and innovation to be combined.

What would it take for a school to resemble BAR racing, capable of dealing with that degree of complexity, innovation and tailoring? It would require good information, sound discipline and shared purpose and an ability to shift resources and change track midstream. Of course BAR has advantages: lots of resources and a highly skilled team of craftsmen and designers. They can test new innovations thoroughly before trying them out. There are limits to how far the BAR approach could be applied to a school. But in principle rather than churning out standardised products, personalised learning in schools might be more like BAR.

Indeed one reason why more affluent parents might be leaving the school system in favour of home schooling – in the US in particular – is to provide more tailored, bespoke services for their children. Even in countries where full-home schooling is uncommon, extra curricular coaching, teaching, courses, and self-motivated learning are likely to become more common, as parents seek to provide elements of personalised services for their children as an adjunct to the standard school system. Personalisation as tailored services is likely to grow as an alternative to standardised education systems (home schooling) and as a complement to them (out-of-school-hours programmes). Nevertheless it seems likely that the school system itself, collective provision of one kind or another, will remain at the core of education for the foreseeable future.

Mass customisation

That means a second approach to personalisation will be mass customisation, in which users are allowed a degree of choice over how to mix and blend standardised components and modules to create a learning programme more suited to their goals. Again, there are good models for this from the private sector. Leading manufacturers such as Dell and Toyota, for example, have well honed just-in-time production systems, which allow users a say in putting together the product mix they want. This is personalisation as choice among a limited range of commodity options provided by a limited range of producers. Such a system already seems to be developing in higher education in some countries, such as the UK, with the introduction of student grants and the creation of a more open market, in which different institutions and programmes can easily be compared. The implication is that personalisation means mass customisation, learners become consumers.

Consumer choice is a good thing in markets that trade goods and services where property rights are relatively clear, products are relatively easy to compare, consumers can gather information easily and there are many buyers and sellers of services. Consumer choice sends signals about what people want so that producers should organise themselves around it. In theory at least, this means that resources can be reallocated to reflect consumer demand rather than reflecting what producers decide should be made. Consumers who are well-informed, able to express clear preferences, and easily exercise those choices in the market are the arbiters of value.

Providing users with greater choice would shake up the public sector by unlocking user aspirations and ambitions. In some services it makes sense to put consumers directly in charge of commissioning the service they want, especially where consumers have far greater knowledge than professionals about what they need and what might be available. To make that a reality in schooling would mean financial flows following choices made by parents and children and much better information for users to compare differences in performance between schools. Capacity would need to shift in response to demand: organisations that became more successful and popular would need to be able to increase their available capacity to meet demand, otherwise queues would just lengthen.

Consumer choice would be a challenge to the power of professionals and providers to allocate resources to services. But the extent to which public services can be driven by consumer choice also has limits. Consumerism works where goods and services can be packaged and priced. Yet education cannot always be neatly packaged in the way that stereos, cars and computers can be. Many public services are fuzzy, difficult to define and pin down, for example the value of community safety. The qualities of these public goods cannot be assessed and encapsulated in the way that the features of a computer can be described in technical language.

Consumerism is based, at least in theory, on individual preferences. But in education it is often difficult to separate one individual's preferences from another's. Parents choose schools in part based on what other parents do. Simplistic models of consumer choice fail to take into account these social and environmental factors. Consumerism works when consumers have good information about service performance. But in the public sector most information, and the ability to interpret it, is in the hands of professionals and staff. Users rarely have all the information they need – about possible costs and benefits of different forms of health treatment for example – to make a fully informed decision. As choice expands so the costs of searching across competing offers rise. As diversity expands so it becomes more difficult to compare different services. Choice imposes costs on consumers as well as benefits.

Market consumerism applied to public services could threaten the principles of equity on which public services are based. Public service goods like health and education are essential to the quality of people's lives and their ability to play a full role in society. These foundational goods should not be distributed by ability to pay but according to need.

Further extension of choice – mass customisation – seems inevitable in school systems coping with diverse needs and demands. But given the difficulties involved, choice cannot provide a sole organising principle for a reform strategy. Users of public services want to be treated well, as customers, but that does not necessarily mean they want to become consumers, shopping around for the best deal or even threatening to do so. We need to find a way to make public services responsive without turning the public sector into a shopping mall. We need a way for users to be treated with respect and consideration when they cannot exercise the sanction of taking their business to another supplier. Moreover even when people have choice that does not mean they are necessarily more satisfied with the outcome they get. I have a wide choice of banks to go to but that does not mean I get a better service from the bank I am already at. Consumers do not just want choice; they want attention to their particular needs. They want voice and support as well as choice among commodities. They want to be treated with respect and care, not just efficient transactions.

Mass-personalisation

That is where a third idea of personalisation comes in: personalisation as participation and co-creation of value. The standard account of value creation is that value is created through transactions. A company creates a product which it owns and then exchanges that product for money. The exchange anoints the product with value and the price measures that value. This transactional view of value creation can work, in amended form in the public sector as well, with services delivered free at the point of delivery. Much of traditional education has been based on this transactional model of value creation: teachers download their knowledge to children and in the transfer value is created and measured by qualifications and exam results.

But this transactional account is only one version of how value is created. Another is that it is often co-created between users and producers: it is not a transactional process but an interactive and participatory one. The underlying idea here is that services are created by scripts. Our models of production and consumption are still dominated by industrially produced goods – cars, stereos, washing machines – the physical and technical characteristic of which can be easily defined and compared. Shopping around for a washing machine in the basement of a department store involves comparing fairly standardised goods. Our images of what it means to be a consumer are still dominated by this shopping mall idea of choosing between different physical goods.

This model is inappropriate for many services. True, more services are now standardised: witness telephone banking or fast food restaurants. But services that generate personal satisfaction or solve personal problems – whether public or private – are far more difficult to define in quantitative terms. It is difficult to shop around for something that cannot be defined easily and to be effective has to be designed with you in mind.

Services should be seen as scripts. All services are delivered according to a script, which directs the parts played by the actors involved. The script for eating a meal in a restaurant is: reserve table; arrive at restaurant and be shown to table; examine menu; place order with waiter; food delivered to table; eat; ask for bill; pay; leave. Service innovation comes from rewriting scripts like this so the action unfolds in a different way. A fast-food restaurant runs on a different script: read menu, place order for food, pay, take food to table yourself, eat, clear away your debris, leave. In a full-service restaurant you eat and then pay, and do very little else. In a fast food restaurant you pay and then eat, and contribute some of your labour by taking the food to the table and clearing away your mess.

Most service innovation comes from producers and users simultaneously adopting a new script, playing out new and complementary roles in the story. It is very difficult for service producers to innovate unless the users also adopt the new roles in the script. Increasingly innovation comes from consumers deciding to write new roles in their script for themselves and insisting that the producers respond. That is the story of the rise of SMS messaging. Mobile phone companies had a script for how SMS messaging would be used: in emergencies. But teenage users of mobile phones invented a new script and with it a new service and new uses for mobile phones. The producers have had to respond to the script that was collectively written by the users. Service innovation is invariably a joint production combining producers and consumers.

Often radical innovation involves bringing together ideas from quite different scripts: the telephone service script (used in banking) and health care knowledge, when brought together created a new script for accessing health advice in the form of NHS Direct. The old script was: phone GP; make appointment; visit surgery. Now there is a new script, which starts with phone call to NHS Direct asking for help. Many of the scripts followed by public services – such as schooling – have not changed for decades: enter classroom; sit at desk; listen to teacher; read from blackboard; write in exercise book; hand in work; run to playground. The scripts for user engagement with the police, health services and libraries, are largely written by professionals, producers and regulators, not by users. The users are expected to fit into the roles given to them by the script handed down from on high.

There are now emerging new organisational models for co-creation on a mass basis: mass personalisation as opposed to mass customisation. Take the Sims online gaming community. The Sims, one of the most ubiquitous and successful computer games ever created, is a prime example of the power of shared authorship. The Sims is a localised version of Sim City, which allows people to design a city and watch it grow, prosper, decline and collapse. The Sims translates this to the neighbourhood and the family. The players can create their own family home and watch the inhabitants sleep, eat, argue, marry, make love, fight and die: a bit like a computer game version of Big Brother.

Before the online version of the game was made available the designers released tools that allowed players to create their own content for the game: furniture, accessories, even architectural styles for houses. By the time the game was launched at least 50 pro-am (innovative, committed, networked amateurs working to professional standards) web sites were already up and running offering these specially crafted items that players could integrate into their own games. Within a year of release there were hundreds of independent content creators, more than 200 fan web sites displaying more than half a million collectable items available to the game's millions of players. More than 90% of the content in the Sims game is now created by a pro-am sector of the Sims playing community. One pro-am site that gives people tools to make their own edgings to put around rugs has had more than 400 000 downloads.

The Sims is successful not just because it is a cleverly designed product, devised by its creators and shipped to a waiting audience. It is also a set of tools – which can be used by competent games players not just hard-core geeks – and it is a shared space in which this collaborative activity takes place. Knowledge about the Sims is not just held in the heads of its original designers who have codified and shipped that know-how to a waiting audience. The Sims community is a distributed, bottom-up, self-organising body of knowledge, in which players are constantly training one another and innovating. Mastering a computer game used to be an individualistic activity undertaken by boys in the dark of their bedrooms. Now it's a mass team sport which depends on intense collaboration.

There is a sound commercial logic behind this open approach to innovation amongst games companies. Open, mass innovation allows many innovations to continue in parallel once a game has been released amongst a distributed community of pro-am players. They also spread good ideas like apostles. Games publishers then get access to a large, unpaid R&D workforce. If a game sells 1 million copies and just 1% of the players are pro-am developers, this means that an R&D team of 10 000 people is working on further developments. Their contributions make the game more interesting and that in turn extends the game's life, constantly refreshing it. As players are then likely to play the game for longer, they are more likely to tell other gamers about their obsession.

This is a model of personalisation as community co-creation of value. Some of the most potent new organisational models – E-Bay, Linux, on-line games – are emerging from organisations that harness the power of communities of co-creation, in which users are also teachers, co-contributors, critics and product developers.

Personalisation through participation

Personalisation through participation makes the connection between the individual and the collective by allowing users a more direct, informed and creative say in rewriting the script by which the service they use is designed, planned, delivered and evaluated. This invariably involves the following steps:

- *Intimate consultation*: professionals working with clients to help unlock their needs, preferences and aspirations, through an extended dialogue.

- *Expanded choice*: giving users greater choice over the mix of ways in which their needs might be met, to assemble solutions around the needs of the user rather than limiting provision to what the institution in question – the school, hospital, social services department – offers.

- *Enhanced voice*: expanded choice should help to further unlock the user's voice. Making comparisons between alternatives helps people to articulate their preferences. This is very difficult to do from a blank sheet of paper. Choice helps to unlock voice.

- *Partnership provision*: it is only possible to assemble solutions personalised to individual need if services work in partnership. An institution – for example a secondary school – should be a gateway to a range of learning offers provided not just by the school but by other local schools, companies, colleges and distance learning programmes. Institutions should be gateways to networks of public provision.

- *Advocacy*: professionals should act as advocates for users, helping them to navigate their way through the system. That means clients having a continuing relationship with professionals who take an interest in their case, rather than users engaging in a series of disconnected transactions with disconnected services.

- *Co-production*: users who are more involved in shaping the service they receive should be expected to become more active and responsible in helping to deliver the service: involved patients are more likely to attend clinics, students to do homework. Personalisation should create more involved, responsible users.

- *Funding*: should follow the choices that users make and in some cases – direct payments to disabled people to assemble their own care packages

– funding should be put in the hands of users themselves, to buy services with the advice of professionals.

Users should not be utterly dependent upon the judgements of professionals; they can question, challenge and deliberate with them. Nor are users mere consumers, choosing between different packages offered to them: they should be more intimately involved in shaping and even co-producing the service they want. Through participation users have greater voice in shaping the service but this is exercised where it counts – where services are designed and delivered. Service users can only change their role in the service script, however, if professionals alter theirs. Professionals have to become advisers, advocates, solutions assemblers, brokers. The role of professionals in participative services is often not to provide solutions directly, but to help clients find the best way to solve their problems themselves.

Personalisation will make sense most in services which are face to face and based on long-term relationships, and which demand direct engagement between professionals and users where the user can play a significant role in shaping the service. This kind of deep personalisation will also make sense in areas where users can increasingly self-provide with only partial reliance on professionals. The ultimate version of personalisation is self-provision and self-creation, not just a personalised service.

Personalised learning should provide children with a greater repertoire of possible scripts for how their education could unfold. At the core there might still be a common script – the basic curriculum – but that script could branch out in many different ways, to have many different styles and endings. The foundation would be to encourage children, from an early age and across all backgrounds, to become more involved in making decisions about what they would like to learn and how. The more aware people are of what makes them learn, the more effective their learning is likely to be.

Young people are far more avid and aware consumers than they used to be. This culture is bound to have an effect on how they view education. Many secondary school age children now have mobile phones for which they can get 24/7 telephone support, different price plans, equipment and service packages. They are used to a world in which they can search for, download and share digital music on the Internet. Children have quite different kinds of aptitude and intelligence, which need to be developed in quite different ways. The school system already recognises that some children have "special" needs and so need personalised kinds of learning environments and teaching styles. But up to now the system as a whole has been unable to deliver this flexibility consistently for all those who need it, or to integrate children with special needs into the "mainstream".

Personalised learning would extend this principle, already implicit in the system, to all children. Equity cannot be handed down from on high in a society with a democratic culture in which people want a say in shaping their lives. Comprehensives promoted equity through common standards. "Personalised learning" allows individual interpretations of the goals and value of education. Children should be able to tell their own story of what they have learned, how and why, as well as being able to reel off their qualifications, the formal hurdles they have overcome. Their personal involvement in making choices about what they learn, how and what targets they set for themselves, would turn them into more active learners.

Personalised learning as mass personalisation rather than mass customisation does not apply market thinking to education. It is not designed to turn children and parents into consumers of education. The aim is to promote personal development through self-realisation, self-enhancement and self-development. The child/learner should be seen as active, responsible and self-motivated, a co-author of the script which determines how education is delivered.

Personalised learning starts from the premise that learners should be actively, continually engaged in setting their own targets, devising their own learning plans and goals, choosing from among a range of different ways to learn. New approaches to assessment, for example "assessment for learning", help learners work out how effective their learning was, what worked well or badly for them. That allows students to adjust and adapt their learning strategies. Traditional assessment tests the extent of someone's knowledge at the end of a period of learning and provides the learner with little information about which learning strategies were more effective. Personalised learning would only work if students were engaged in continual, self-critical assessment of their talents, performance, learning strategies and goals.

Personalised learning would allow and encourage learning to take place during holidays and outside normal schools hours. It would make opportunities to learn available whenever the learner wanted to take them up. Children would be able to take time out for other activities that might add to their learning: voluntary work, drama and sports. This flexibility might be based on the principle of "earned autonomy". Children who clearly do well and are self motivated become more self regulating. Students could have a choice – under earned autonomy – about where learning takes place: at home; at an individual school; moving among a network of schools; virtually through ICT in school, at home or in a third space such as a library; *in situ* at a workplace or voluntary group.

What mass-personalisation means for schools and teachers?

A mass, personalised learning service would be revolutionary. By giving learners a growing voice, their aspirations and ambitions would become central to the way services were organised. At the moment the heart of the system are its institutions and professions – teachers and schools – that lay down what education is and how it should proceed. Studies of performance management across a wide range of organisational fields show that productivity invariably rises when people have a role in setting and thus owning their targets. The same is true for learning.

This implies far-reaching changes in the role of professionals and schools. Schools would become solution-assemblers, helping children get access to the mix and range of learning resources they need, both virtual and face-to-face. Schools would have to form networks and federations which shared resources and centres of excellence. An individual school in the network would become a gateway to these shared resources. What does this mean for funding of education? Should each school get a set sum per child? Should the money follow the student? Should every student have an amount they can spend on learning materials from outside the school? All these options have complications. Yet if money does not flow with student choices then the system will not be truly responding to learner demand.

The biggest challenge to the personalised learning agenda is what it means for inequality. Take the case of personalised learning. Middle class homes are often far more conducive to personalised learning than many poorer homes that have less space, fewer computers and books. Thus the more that personalised learning promotes self-provisioning, the more it could widen inequalities. As more learning would be done in the pupil's own time, so the state would have to work harder to equalise the conditions for learning outside school. Personalised learning will promote equity only if the resources for individualised, home-based learning are also more equally available. Personalised learning encourages us to focus on the totality of resources available for learning, at home and at school. Linking schools to family services, nurseries and children's' trusts will be vital to better prepare children from all backgrounds to take advantage of opportunities for personalised learning.

Middle class children do not just have more resources for learning; they and their parents probably have more time and capacity to make choices about education. Choices are made in a social context of peer and family influences. If these mitigate against learning – for example if parents had a negative experience of school, or elder siblings left school with few qualifications – then providing kids from poor, chaotic or disrupted families with *more* choice may not encourage them to consider *different* choices.

Culturally and emotionally nourished children will see huge opportunities in personalised education; those who do not come from these backgrounds may not recognise the choices available to them.

The more that services become personalised, then, the more that public resources will have to be skewed towards the least well off to equalise opportunities. Well-educated and informed consumers are already well prepared to take advantage of choice. The least well educated, informed and ambitious will need additional help to exploit the opportunities personalisation makes available to them.

Conclusion

A chasm has opened up between people and large organisations, both public and private. Many people's experience of being consumers is that they are put on hold, kept at arms length, not told the whole story, tricked by the fine print, redirected to a website and treated like a number. We feel detached from large organisations public and private that serve us in increasingly impersonal ways. While choice among commodity goods and services has expanded, the scope for personalised, human service, tailored to one's needs, seems to have declined.

This gap between large organisations and the intricacy of people's everyday expectations and aspirations is a breeding ground for a growing sense of frustration and resentment, with private services as much as public. This chasm should also be the breeding ground for innovation and experimentation. That is what personalisation is about: finding innovative ways to reconnect people to the institutions that serve them, in this case the education system.

The debate about the future of public services is pitched into this chasm between the way public institutions work and how users experience them. Targets, league tables and inspection regimes may have improved aspects of performance in public services. Yet the cost has been to make public services seem more machine-like, more like a production line producing standardised goods. The aim of personalised learning is not to provide the self-interested with the self-gratification of consumerism but to build a sense of self-actualisation, self-realisation and self-enhancement. The more people are involved in making decisions about services, the more knowledgeable they become, and the more responsible and committed they become to making sure the service is a success.

Across a range of activities it is increasingly clear that the state cannot deliver collective solutions from on high. It is too cumbersome and distant. The state can only help create public goods – like better education and health – by encouraging them to emerge from within society. This is true for health, education, community safety, neighbourhood renewal and a range of other public goods.

Public policy is most effective when it harnesses and shapes private activity rather than supplanting it, allowing the public good to emerge from within civil society. Personalised services are one point in a range of different ways in which public and private work together to create the public good. The state's job will be to orchestrate and enable that process, not to pretend it can provide or deliver all the solutions in the form of discrete services.

The challenge then is not just to personalise services but to shift from a model in which the centre controls, initiates, plans, instructs, serves to one in which the centre governs through promoting collaborative, critical and honest self-evaluation and self-improvement. Reforms to public services should drive in this direction promoting new sources of information for users, creating new interfaces like NHS Direct for them to access services and get advice, providing professionals with the skills and support to become brokers and advisers as well as solutions providers, changing funding regimes to give users more influence over how money is spent on the service they consumer, giving users a right to voice in the design of the services they use.

A state that is committed to protecting the private freedom must also continuously shape how people use their freedom in the name of the wider public good. Personalisation through participation is part of the solution to this dilemma of how to rule through freedom, to allow the public good to be created within society rather than relying on the state to deliver it.

Chapter 8
Personalisation: Getting the Questions Right

by

Tom Bentley and Riel Miller[*]

Personalisation, argue the authors, promises to overcome the uneven results of educational delivery and link innovation in the public sector to the broader transformations in OECD societies. It is not purely a function of choice between alternative supply channels, but of shaping and combining different learning resources and sources of support around personal progression. Bentley and Miller discuss the personalisation divides – demand/supply, public/private. They describe entry points to system-wide change through different questions and issues: universal? diverse? transparent?; learning and teaching – the role of the active learner; learning beyond the classroom – the role of communities; reshaping roles and the workforce; organisation and coordination. The system-wide shift that personalisation could help to stimulate, they conclude, has the potential to be as profound as any transition that public education systems have undertaken before, but this requires both a compelling political narrative and a strategy for distributed change.

The goal

"High excellence, high equity" is the phrase used by David Miliband and David Hopkins to capture the challenge for the next phases of education reform. While universal education has long been an aspiration in the industrialised world, its delivery has also reflected and sometimes entrenched existing patterns of socio-economic inequality. Personalisation may be a way to overcome the uneven results of educational delivery and

---

[*] Respectively, Director of the think-tank Demos, London, *www.demos.co.uk*; and Associate, Demos, London, and Senior Visiting Fellow, Danish Technological Institute.

link innovation in the public sector to the broader transformations taking place in OECD societies.

This is why personalisation, as a new strategic focus for public sector reform, merits careful study. As an approach to making good on the promise of universal education personalisation carries a dual ambition. One is to build an agenda to *make personalised learning a practical reality* through strategic innovation and leadership. The second, on which the first ultimately depends, is to discover the links and innovations that integrate educational reform with the broader context of *public services, governance and long term change in society.*

Political strategies reflect the evolving perceptions and aspirations of citizens, and the limits and abilities of our current institutions. Most political promises of the last generation have sought to improve the institutions we have; better schools, hospitals, pensions and so on. But lasting, transformative change also depends on the emergence of new institutions and practices that harness deeper social forces. This chapter, and the book it is part of, explore how and where personalisation might fit.

Education is a particularly useful proving ground for the potential of personalisation policies because of its political salience, but also because most people believe that learning will be a key ingredient of a successful post-industrial society or economy. Schooling systems are already in flux, and the expectations and practices of teachers, pupils and parents are also moving fast. Reforms which make personalised learning a practical reality for all learners, where ever and when ever they learn, could have a much broader impact. This agenda should be seen as an attempt to understand how our collective efforts can better serve our collective aspirations.

Recent movement

The standards and benchmarking movements of the 1990s reflected a determination to overcome the legacy of low expectations and class-based inequality in education, with a special emphasis on achieving the basics in order to equip most children with the competencies and knowledge they needed to access the full school curriculum.

Despite the emphasis on consistency and informed prescription, however, these policies always co-existed with movement towards a more diverse schooling system. The emphasis on diversity – through *specialisation, curriculum flexibility* and a more *prominent role for choice –* reflects both reality and aspiration; the reality of a more diverse society with a growing range of learner talents, and the expectation that the pressure for responsiveness from individual learners and families will continue to grow.

The attempt to combine this responsiveness with shared public settings which maintain norms of fairness, contribution and reciprocity is important for the future of all public services.

Personalisation is not purely a function of choice between alternative supply channels, therefore, but of shaping and combining many different learning resources and sources of support around personal progression. It has radical consequences for many aspects of our current system. But those consequences are uncharted, precisely because they depend on the interaction of many different factors.

Personalisation divides: demand-side/supply-side, public/private

Personalisation means that a good or service reflects the needs and attributes of the individual. There are many different ways to meet this objective. The predominant way in OECD countries is to wait for a producer of the good or service to adapt the offer. More often than not this has meant a passive role for the consumer who, though sovereign in their "right to choose", still selects from a fixed set of options.

Following this path towards personalisation would mean supplier institutions defining and categorising new options. But there is an alternative path; one which *integrates* the invention and production of personalised output, so that the user (learner) is directly involved in both the design and the creation of the learning experience and outcome. Both of these paths are currently being pursued. For example schools are attempting to become more specialised, while learners (and their parents) try to detail their needs and expectations more clearly.

Another key dividing line is between public and private. For instance, personalisation efforts in the public sector have typically unfolded without many of the pressures and adaptations typical of private markets. Some argue that public sector institutions, lacking competitive mechanisms of success, failure, investment and disinvestment, will find it difficult to personalise. The idea of personalised learning may also challenge the power of those systems, including schooling, that define and certify what is considered legitimate knowledge. Demand-led personalisation therefore threatens some forms of institutional self-preservation.

These public-private tensions compound the challenge of distinguishing between the different forces that drive personalisation on the supply- and demand-sides. But they also create a very wide range of possible outcomes or future forms for education systems. Public education cannot simply be reduced to consumer flexibility, but personalisation creates new opportunities to examine the boundaries of shared knowledge and social norms and their role in shaping the broader public realm.

A range of personalisation prospects

One ironic outcome of private sector firms' experiences with "mass-customisation" has been the response of consumers to the immense range of choices they were offered. Much to the surprise of the managers who led the huge investments necessary to offer mass-customisation, in most cases consumers selected from within a narrow range. For instance two renowned manufacturers, Cannondale, a specialty bicycle manufacturer, and Motorola, the electronics firm, geared up in the 1990s to provide consumers with millions of options. Cannondale was able to configure over 8 million different frame and colour variations for its bicycles. Motorola also succeeded in making its Bravo pagers available in millions of possible shapes and colours (Wind and Rangaswamy 1999). Today, both companies sell an impressive range of products through traditional retail channels, neither offers millions of variations on demand.

Personalisation of education might generate the same outcome; if expectations of educational experience remain static, the broadening of options by schools may not in itself lead to more diverse forms of learning. Instead, personalised education might offer a "just in time" approach which put together separate modules to reflect the needs of a particular individual learner, but left the underlying modules of learning, curriculum content and so on as standard and "factory produced". A personalised system offers a bigger, more diverse catalogue to the informed shopper. Arguably, this is best practice for schools and companies today. What other possibilities can we imagine?

Imagine a catalogue that consists of items you invent, design and conceive yourself and the supplier is more of an assistant who connects up with you momentarily through a vast, continuously reconfigured network. This does not just build on the century old model of the mail order catalogue if it takes us beyond the static and passive position of the consumer. In this post-industrial catalogue, which the "producer-consumer" or *prosumer* can publish as their personalised version others might then build on, the crucial ingredient is the value added by the individual themselves. Their capacity to invent, design and then co-produce is what distinguishes this version of personalisation from mass-customisation.

The prospects for this type of personalisation do not seem so far fetched for people who are using the Internet to stitch together and produce their own news, entertainment and markets. Blogs, e-bay type auction spaces, web portals that aggregate information based on user generated profiles, all of these developments hint at an alternative, more joined-up or coincident relationship between supply and demand (see for example *www.demosgreenhuse.co.uk*).

Imagine an Internet portal that you own and control and that contains your health records, financial assets, work achievements, clothing designs, furniture plans, music mixes, multiple levels of networks for: friends, acquaintances, colleagues, entertainment, debate, local action, global voting. In this personal gateway to the world everything is organised according to your needs rather than how institutions package, own or credential things. This version of future post-industrial personalisation moves past the need for fixed categories and product boundaries through which to exercise choice, and builds on a fluid, self-organising model which is capable of generating more spontaneous responses to articulated need. Learning is at its core because learning is the source of personalisation. Only it is not the learning related to meeting the requirements of a test set by someone else, but learning that is motivated, acquired and expressed through personalisation.

Current ambitions for reform, public or private, do not target the prospect of a post-industrial world. More common is the strong opposition elicited by even modest hints at alternative approaches, like the emerging "open source" and "copy left" movements. That is why it is useful, as part of an effort to understand why and how to advance personalisation in education, to consider the prospect of versions that go beyond extrapolations rooted in the industrial past.

Institutional constraints

As we have argued elsewhere, our school systems offer a trade-off between different goods (Bentley, 1998). They are not always designed for optimal learning, but they are mostly reliable and secure. They are not accessible for all learners at all times, but during the 20th century they represented a cost-effective way to get almost all children through a basic educational threshold. They have not always generated deep understanding and love of learning, but they have trained generations of young people in the rules and rhythms of industrial organisation.

Most teachers, parents and learners would surely agree that a system which responds to personal need, motivation and progression is desirable. Most would also be able to point to some aspect of the current system – good teaching, individual learning profiles, choices at key moments – which personalise the experience. In that sense, we can see glimpses of the future in our current practices. But how might they combine? Is it possible to imagine a system capable of personalising the learning experience and progression of *every* student? How are such capabilities developed?

But, in important respects, our current systems of

- institutional structure,
- funding,
- regulation,
- measurement,
- entitlement and
- political choice

set limits on the extent to which personalisation can be universalised.

Entry points to system-wide change

One challenge for the evolution of the debate, then, is to identify how a strategy can unlock the potential for greater personalisation by getting different components of the system to work together more productively, while also generating innovations that could change it more radically over time. We can already spell out many of the ingredients of personalised learning or public services, at least in the short term, but we do not yet fully know how to combine them in a successful recipe.

The rest of this paper aims to identify questions about the ingredients of system-wide change; not just what they are, but also how they occur, as a contribution to a fuller discussion of personalisation policies.

Universal?

The first major challenge concerns how to ensure that personalisation is not dominated by those who are better off and most able to dominate selective or voluntary opportunities. Entitlement has provided the justification for various strong features of the current system, including the compulsory nature of schooling itself and the rigidities of the curriculum, or at least those parts considered essential. This begs the question: if personalised learning is to become universal, how can it engage most effectively with those who have most to gain from it?

Another way of expressing this question is: How should an entitlement to personalised learning be expressed? How could it be guaranteed? For example, the public debate over the use of standards and numerical targets has developed in the UK into a broader discussion of how quality standards and qualitative experiences can form part of successful improvement strategies, alongside the hard, easily measured objectives.

An entitlement to personalised learning might not take the form of a guaranteed school place or age-specific numeracy level, but of an allocation of resources, of access to an advocate, or of a direct voice and responsibility in certain decisions. A universal institutional experience, in other words, might over time become universal participation in a far more fluid system which combines formal and informal learning around a personal pathway.

Diverse?

If personalisation is a reflection of social and learner diversity, then what forms of diversity should a personalised system encompass? At the moment, diversity is being introduced into the school system in several ways, but the most powerful – specialisation – assumes *subject* diversity while leaving every other aspect of schooling and its organisation in a standard form.

Diversity can be expressed in many other ways:

- The diversity of organisations involved in providing learning opportunities, their location and form.

- The diversity of learners and their intelligence profiles.

- The range of choice available to each student or family at a given time.

- The range of practices or possible responses each provider is capable of – the range of learning possibilities within a given organisation.

But the extent to which diversity reflects genuine differences in learning and progression remains a matter of contention.

So, for example, what changes to our qualification and award systems are needed to reflect what we are now learning about the range of human intelligence and the forms of attainment that a 21st century society will value? What kind of assessment methods and infrastructures are needed to recognise a more diverse range of learning activities? How might digitisation of assessment records and procedures play a role here?

Transparent? The role of data

Personalising the learning experience depends on teachers and learners being able to tailor provision to progression. Doing so for all students depends on the quality of information with which to make such decisions. Good teachers will constantly be making intuitive and on-the-spot decisions about how to adjust pace, content, questions and rewards according to differences among the learners in front of them. But again, the prospect of universal personalisation goes far beyond this use of information.

The English school system has already seen the introduction of individual student profiles which allow personalised data collection, comparison of attainment against benchmarks, individual teacher planning and evaluation, and more detailed record keeping by schools. But how do the possibilities of a personalised system impact on the nature of data collection and management by other agencies? At what point should relevant learner information be compiled? How does student information contribute to school performance information and officially maintained datasets? We know from past experience the powerful shaping effect that performance information has on organisational behaviour.

We would suggest that pursuing the skills of independent learner effectiveness and developing strategies for formative assessment present the most immediate opportunities to move towards personalisation.

These questions, though, only address the framework of existing institutions. Transparency and access to a wider infrastructure of learning rests on issues such privacy and ownership of personal data, and the ability to validate or authenticate one's own identity in order to access learning resources or collaborate with others.

One way to picture such a capability is to imagine being able to use existing educational facilities as entry points to much wider networks of flexible, specialist, provision and participation. What expectations and connections would need to be in place for this to be an everyday reality? How do different kinds of learning demand and achievement attain visibility and reliable evaluation alongside our current forms of measurement?

Learning and teaching: the role of the active learner

The debate on personalisation also reflects the radical change that our understanding of learning has already gone through over the last generation. Our historical assumptions about the fixed, general nature of intelligence and learning ability are gradually giving way to a far more fluid and fiercely contested view. We know that the years *before* compulsory education are probably most influential in determining prospects for formal attainment and perhaps also appetite for learning. We know that there are multiple forms of intelligence, and that they can be stimulated and developed in a wide range of ways.

We are beginning to learn the effects and influences of different cognitive processes – brain function – on the habits of mind and ability to learn. Yet little of this knowledge has been applied systematically to the practices of teaching or educational management (Demos, 2005). How far should this be part of a move towards personalisation? How confident can we be about the findings of cognitive science?

Beyond this knowledge base lies a series of fundamental questions about pedagogy and the role of the learner. Personalisation must surely revolve around teaching and learning, but the implication of a system organised around the most powerful learning experiences and the tailored progression of each student is a different role, and voice, for the learner in the whole process. In a personalised system, *engagement* acquires a fundamental importance alongside attainment and progression. It does not replace knowledge or understanding, but the active involvement, shared ownership, motivation and self-discipline of the learner becomes a foundation on which the whole system operates.

Such a system might create very different patterns of engagement:

- Starting in the early years education might focus more explicitly on developing a range of abilities and creating foundations for successful later learning.

- Family and formal learning might become more closely integrated.

- Learner records and self assessment might become a more formative and explicit part of educational planning.

- Learning how to learn might become an explicit objective of public education, integrated into other aspects of the curriculum.

- Crucial junctions, or choice points in an educational career might be supported by a range of information, guidance and collaboration going far beyond the current institutional frameworks.

Learning beyond the classroom: the role of communities

Partnership and support beyond the classroom play a crucial role in the current vision of personalisation. From extended learning provision to home-school partnership, mentoring to work-based learning, a range of community resources act as powerful supports for educational attainment. It may also be that learning in authentic and voluntary settings, through relationships which are not formalised in the same manner as those of the school, adds force to the motivation and depth of the learning experience.

We know how much factors such parental involvement, peer group, community expectations and home-based learning resources make a difference to educational achievement. Many different ways to harness them creatively have opened up over the last decade. How would they be involved systematically in a personalised education framework?

These issues go far beyond education in their importance. All public services strive to create public goods which enable people to live their own lives better – all are reinforced by voluntary behaviours which strengthen those goods: exercise and diet for health, nurture and care for children and elders, and so on. The spaces between formal public provision and private individuals – expressed through voluntary networks, mutual partnerships, public conversations and so on – are very often the spaces through which new institutions or large scale practices can emerge. Education currently has numerous cross cutting arrangements of this kind – as do other sectors. Developing and evaluating the new forms of governance required to create value from these lateral partnerships is therefore a priority in many systems.

Reshaping roles and workforce

Effective schooling has revolved for at least a generation around a highly coordinated and disciplined model of workforce organisation; a single head teacher providing integrated leadership, responsibilities and subjects broken into hierarchical departments, a strong team ethos and a system of continuous professional development and incremental improvement. In recent years, this familiar structure has begun to give way at the edges, as a result of both policy and of unplanned innovation. The rigid distinction between teachers as professionals and other learning support workers has eroded: para-professional roles are now familiar in classrooms, and a host of other support and advisory roles has sprung up.

But how might personalised learning reshape the organisational pattern of schooling and other related agencies? Personalised progression, for example, might require a stronger connection between individual student and a professional responsible for their progression. Team teaching might generate a new range of specialist roles and combinations, giving rise to more flexible strategies for learning and teaching across classes.

The role of assessment and curriculum specialists might also change radically with greater emphasis on personal progression across a range of learning contexts, and greater investment in knitting together knowledge from separate subjects and disciplines. The advisory, or "brokerage" role in a personalised system could also be far more prominent, but might involve significant challenge to the current range of professional advisors and support workers potentially available to young people. Responsibility for simplicity, or integration, might become as important as any other specialist knowledge.

Again, this complex set of issues foreshadows an even deeper set of changes across the public service workforce and beyond. They include:

- The growth of flexible employment and new forms of work-life integration.

- Challenges to the established professional model and new kinds of public "knowledge work", using and sharing knowledge in radically different ways to help create value for individuals.

- New career pathways and methods to assess and validate people's competencies.

- Reshaping of labour and knowledge markets to reflect new methods of trading time and competencies, especially using electronic networks (see for example Rowan, 1997).

Organisation and coordination

Finally, a more flexible system built around personalised learning pathways would also present new challenges and opportunities to the organisation of education itself. The current shape of our schools reflects a clear organisation structure built on powerful, enduring assumptions about learning. The evolution of a regulatory infrastructure which strengthens command and control, manages performance, enforces accountability measures and allocates resources reflects the strength of hierarchical governance structures under certain conditions.

Personalised learning, as it focuses attention on what within the schooling package is most powerful and effective, will generate demands for more responsive and adaptive organisational systems. Knowledge and information will need to move faster and more reliably across different locations and organisational units. Learners and professionals will be more mobile, and may carry far greater volumes of data with them through digital and wireless technology. Flexible patterns of provision will be demanded by the new combinations of modular courses, apprenticeship learning and intensive, specialist learning.

As is already beginning to happen, groups of local providers might share common resources and offer each other access to their specialisms, in order to broaden the range of curriculum choice available. Learner pathways might be planned and mapped across groups of institutions in the same way that "clinical pathways" are now understood by leading edge healthcare providers. A pathway-based approach to progression might also enrol a learner in a local system through a base institution, but not insist on age-group progress at an equal pace in all areas of learning.

Conclusion

The broad questions raised in this paper will be answered not just by analysis and imagination, but by innovation and experimentation. Just as economic systems have moved over the last generation towards more explicit strategies for learning from innovation, embedding such learning in every aspect of the production process, so public and social systems are becoming preoccupied with how to harness, adapt and integrate the outcomes of innovation into their efforts to create public value.

The system-wide shift that personalisation could help to stimulate has the potential to be as profound as any transition that public education systems have undertaken before. To have such an effect, however, requires both a compelling political narrative and a strategy for distributed change. As Charles Leadbeater argues, personalisation has the potential to become a "disruptive" idea because, once absorbed by citizens, it can take on a life of its own, fuelling demand for responsive services and new learning opportunities (2004). The job of politics is to frame this kind of vision in a way that allows it to take root, and connects it with other historical goals which only politics can achieve.

A "shallow" version of personalisation which re-shuffled the existing building blocks of public service production and presented them "just in time" to the user is perfectly possible to envisage. Indeed, certain sectors in certain OECD countries may be already there. A deeper set of changes, however, is clearly occurring around us, and forcing our governance institutions to contemplate new distributions of power, authority and legitimacy. A more transformative agenda for personalisation will place itself firmly amid these changes and seek to shape them for the better.

References

Bentley, T. (1998), "Learning Beyond the Classroom; Education for a Changing World, Routledge, London.

Demos (2005), "About Learning; Report of the Learning Working Group", *www.demos.co.uk*

Leadbeater, C. (2004), "Personalisation through Participation", Demos, London.

Miller, R. and T. Bentley (2003), "Unique Creation: Four Scenarios for the Future of Schooling", NCSL, Nottingham.

Rowan, W. (1997), "Guaranteed Electronic Markets", Demos, London.

Wind, J. and A. Rangaswamy (1999), "Customerization: The Second Revolution in Mass Customization", eBusiness Research Center Working Paper, 06-1999, Penn State, *www.smeal.psu.edu/ebrc/publications/res_papers/1999_06.pdf*

Also available in the CERI collection

Students with Disabilities, Learning Difficulties and Disadvantages – *Statistics and Indicators*
152 pages • October 2005 • ISBN: 92-64-00980-9

E-learning in Tertiary Education: Where do We Stand?
290 pages • June 2005 • ISBN: 92-64-00920-5

Formative Assessment – Improving Learning in Secondary Classrooms
280 pages • February 2005 • ISBN: 92-64-00739-3

Quality and Recognition in Higher Education: The Cross-border Challenge
205 pages • October 2004 • ISBN: 92-64-01508-6

Internationalisation and Trade in Higher Education – *Opportunities and Challenges*
250 pages • June 2004 • ISBN: 92-64-01504-3

Innovation in the Knowledge Economy – *Implications for Education and Learning*
Knowledge Management series
96 pages • May 2004 • ISBN: 92-64-10560-3

Equity in Education – *Students with Disabilities, Learning Difficulties and Disadvantages*
165 pages • May 2004 • ISBN: 92-64-10368-6

www.oecdbookshop.org

OECD PUBLICATIONS, 2, rue André-Pascal, 75775 PARIS CEDEX 16
PRINTED IN FRANCE
(96 2006 03 1 P) ISBN 92-64-03659-8 – No. 54995 2006